# MOUNTAIN RANCH

## AT THE END OF THE ROAD

ISBN-13: 978-0-88839-056-1 [trade edition softcover]
ISBN-13: 978-0-88839-284-8 [epub format]
Copyright © Connie Hook

---

**Library and Archives Canada Cataloguing in Publication**

Title: Mountain ranch at the end of the road : horses, cows, guns and grizzlies in the Canadian wilderness / by Tom Hook ; posthumously compiled and arranged by Gary Brumbelow.
Names: Hook, Tom, 1940-2011, author. | Brumbelow, Gary, editor.
Description: Includes index.
Identifiers: Canadiana 20190056274 | ISBN 9780888390561 (softcover)
Subjects: LCSH: Hook, Tom, 1940-2011. | LCSH: Ranchers—British Columbia—Biography. | LCSH: Ranch life—British Columbia—Anecdotes. | LCSH: Ranching—British Columbia—Anecdotes. | LCGFT: Autobiographies.
Classification: LCC FC3845.C3 H66 2019 | DDC 636.20092—dc23

---

All rights reserved. No part of this publication may be reproduced, stored in a retrieval system or transmitted, in any form or by any means, electronic, mechanical, audio, photocopying, recording, or otherwise (except for copying permitted by Sections 107 and 108 of the U.S. Copyright Law and except for book reviews for the public press), without the prior written permission of Hancock House Publishers. Permissions and licensing contribute to the book industry by helping to support writers and publishers through the purchase of authorized editions and exerpts. Please visit www.accesscopyright.ca.

Illustrations and photographs are copyrighted by the artist or the Publisher.
*Editing by* D. Martens
*Production by* M. Lamont & M. Balignasay
*Cover Illustration* by Don Gill

Printed in the the USA

We acknowledge the financial support of the Government of Canada through the Canada Book Fund and the Canada Council for the Arts, and of the Province of British Columbia through the British Columbia Arts Council and the Book Publishing Tax Credit.

*Hancock House gratefully acknowledges the Semiahmoo, Kwantlen and Katzie First Nations, whose unceded traditional territories our offices reside upon.*

**Published simultaneously in Canada and the United States by**
**HANCOCK HOUSE PUBLISHERS LTD.**
19313 Zero Avenue, Surrey, B.C. Canada V3Z 9R9
(604) 538-1114                Fax (604) 538-2262
**HANCOCK HOUSE PUBLISHERS**
#104-4550 Birch Bay-Lynden Rd, Blaine, WA, U.S.A. 98230-9436
(800) 938-1114                Fax (800) 983-2262
www.hancockhouse.com     sales@hancockhouse.com

# MOUNTAIN RANCH

## AT THE END OF THE ROAD

### BY TOM HOOK

POSTHUMOUSLY COMPILED AND
ARRANGED BY
GARY BRUMBELOW

*HORSES, COWS, GUNS AND GRIZZLIES IN THE CANADIAN WILDERNESS*

# CONTENTS

**PREFACE** ........................................................................ 6
**PROLOGUE** .................................................................... 9

**CHAPTER ONE** - WE DECIDE TO MOVE ..................... 12
**CHAPTER TWO** - BIG MOVE TO A BIG RANCH .... 26
**CHAPTER THREE** - LIFE AT EMPIRE ......................... 34
**CHAPTER FOUR** - RANCHING AT EMPIRE ............... 49
**CHAPTER FIVE** - NEIGHBORS ....................................... 68
**CHAPTER SIX** - THE COWBOYS ................................... 74
**CHAPTER SEVEN** - FIRST NATIONS ........................... 93
**CHAPTER EIGHT** - WILDLIFE ..................................... 108
**EPILOGUE** ................................................................... 126
**APPENDIX A** - RANCHING IN CANADA VS. THE U.S. .... 144
**APPENDIX B** - CATTLE BREEDING & BLOODLINES .... 149
**APPENDIX C** - FRANKLIN NASH ............................... 153
**APPENDIX D** - SURVIVING AT EMPIRE ................... 158
**INDEX** .......................................................................... 162

# PREFACE

Tom Hook was a true modern-day cowboy and rancher who moved his family, cattle, and equipment from Colorado to a rugged, remote area of British Columbia where he had bought a ranch operating on 325,000 acres of wilderness. The headquarters were 80 miles beyond the pavement; his range extended another 75 miles west into the Coast Mountains.

Tom's adventures included punching cows in mountain country with hired hands who were mostly Natives or outlaws, facing hazards that included wolves, grizzly bears, cougars, and eagles. The stories read like fiction, but they are all true.

Tom loved his family, his neighbors, and his cows. He combined a deep respect for people with a good-natured humor. For 32 years it was my privilege to know this prince of a man—a gentleman, leader, adventurer, cattleman, beloved father and husband, and loyal friend to many people all over the West. In every one of those categories he was a giant. I have never known the likes of him and I don't expect to again, a real man's man of humility and courtesy combined with professional expertise. He lived by the code of the West and, from early in his marriage to his delightful Connie, walked with God. These virtues light up his stories, to the delight of those who were reading them on a cattleman's web page where Tom was posting, writing under the pseudonym Idaman. His blog entries, at over 26,000 views at the time, was the top-viewed thread. He filed his final post a few days before he died suddenly on February 8, 2011. Now, at over 150,000 views, the Idaman thread is still No. 1 these seven years later, out of 13,000 topics.

Many of Tom's blog readers asked him to write a book. He wanted to oblige. In late 2010 he approached me about helping him prepare his blog posts for publication. Tom had been a good friend since we first met in October 1978, and I counted it a privilege to work with him on the project.

# PREFACE

Tom Hook and Gary Brumbelow, 1980

We had just got started when he was promoted to glory, an unspeakable joy for Tom but a source of devastating grief to his family and friends. In the years since, Connie graciously picked up his torch to work with me. This book is the fruit of those labors.

The whole time I knew Tom Hook, he had to live at the very end of the road. Empire Valley was the most extreme example of that, as you will read in these pages, but his ranches in central Oregon and Idaho were the same. If you could drive past the place, it wasn't right for him.

Of course, it takes two to pull that off, and in some ways, Connie is even more like Tom than Tom was. My wife and I were touring Denali National Park in Alaska with the Hooks years ago when we came upon a little trapper's cabin, long since abandoned, literally in the middle of the wilderness, a bazillion miles from civilization in the wildest kind of country frequented only by grizzlies, wolves, caribou, and lesser critters. Connie took one look and said, "Now that looks like just about the perfect place to live!"

7

Valerie and I still smile when we think about it. It's one of many warm memories of Tom and Connie Hook. I still miss Tom very much and can't wait to see him again.

I know you will enjoy reading about their unusual life.

—Gary Brumbelow<br>
Boring, Oregon<br>
January 16, 2017

# PROLOGUE

Aranching life on the frontier has its moments. Like the time I almost committed armed robbery. ... At least that's how the clerk saw it.

It was four in the morning and I was punch-drunk from lack of sleep. I had driven to town—2.5 hours over bad gravel roads—with a heifer that badly needed the vet. He had met me at the clinic at 3 a.m. but couldn't help her. Now, I just needed some sleep.

I headed to a nearby motel, staggered in, and woke the desk man. When he came into the office he took one look, raised his hands, and backed against the wall, his eyes gigantic. At first I couldn't figure out what was wrong.

It had been a long day. We were calving heifers, back before we used low calving-weight bulls. We had quite a number of heifers and almost lived with them. That evening a heifer was having difficulties and we put her in a small pen to check her out. I reached inside the heifer and encountered something I had never felt before in all my years of raising cattle. At the front of the pelvis there was a flat wall I couldn't reach around. It angled slightly toward the front of the cow on the right side but did not allow for any further entry. I could tell that what I was feeling was not going to be fixed without surgery.

I had learned to do surgeries some time before and have done several since. My first surgery was on a Saturday; no livestock vet was available. I was guided over the phone by a dog-and-cat vet. We did the best we could, neither of us very confident. But the operation was successful, as both animals lived and the heifer bred back very quickly.

But this case was more ominous than any I had handled, so I knew I had to get her to Williams Lake. I got ready, loaded the heifer, and headed out just as it was turning dark. I was driving a one-ton flatbed truck with a stock rack and duals on the rear. I threw in an extra spare just in case.

I had driven about an hour when a tire blew. I immediately thought, "No problem, I've got an extra spare." I changed the tire and went on. Fifteen minutes later the second tire blew and I repeated the procedure. This was a 20 mph road, so heat wasn't the problem, just sharp rocks.

I went on again, thinking how good it was to have brought two spares. I was still thinking that when the third tire blew. I really scratched my head to figure out the best possible positioning for the five tires I had left. I made the change and went on, but in a somewhat more serious mood now.

Sure enough, after another 15 miles a fourth one blew. Now it was really serious, but I only had 20 more miles to go. I was down to four tires, just one on each corner. The rest of the very nervous trip went okay. At the edge of town I stopped at a pay phone and called the vet, and he met me at the clinic. He operated and found that the calf had started out naturally, but when the front feet hit the front of the pelvis they were deflected down instead of into the pelvis. They had punctured the wall of the uterus right at the pelvis, and the heifer had shoved the calf partially through the puncture and down into the stomach cavity. The calf was half in the uterus and half hanging down into the stomach. The flat wall I had felt from the rear was the side of the ribs as the heifer had shoved the calf up sideways against the front of the pelvis.

The vet took the calf out, but it was dead. He tried to sew up the tear in the cow's pelvis. The tear was so far up and under the lower lip of the pelvis he couldn't achieve a very good repair.

That's when I got back in the truck and drove to a motel. I staggered in and hit the bell, only to have the clerk react like I was about to shoot him. I had to look around to see what had spooked him so badly. Then I saw it: my .30-30 rifle on the counter. I was so punchy I forgot I'd laid it there. And the poor clerk thought he was being robbed.

I reassured him that all was well and I just wanted a room. He finally calmed down and checked me in but kept his free hand on the phone until I headed for my room.

The truck I had driven to town was the one the cowboys used every day, so it always had a rifle on board. I must have thought clearly enough to take the rifle in so it wouldn't get stolen, but not clearly

## PROLOGUE

enough to anticipate its effect on the desk man. He put me in a back room well away from the office.

In the morning I found out the heifer was dead also, so the whole episode had only two purposes: an unforgettable experience, and the determination to find a better way of calving heifers. When you're operating in the mountains, at the end of the road, two and a half hard hours from town ... well, let's just say you have to get creative.

The distance from town was the determining factor.

That was one of many memorable experiences during our years at Empire Valley Ranch.

## CHAPTER ONE

# WE DECIDE TO MOVE

For the first thirteen years of our marriage, Connie and I ranched in Colorado at the base of the Sangre de Cristos mountains.

Colorado ranch headquarters

The place had been in the Hook family since 1864. In the early days of ranching in south central Colorado, cattle were actually very secondary to the operation of a ranch. The main income center was the production and sale of horse hay. From some old records I can see that hay sold for as much as $100 per ton, about what it is today. (Think of

# WE DECIDE TO MOVE

the difference in the profit picture with today's cost of production versus that of 120 years ago!)

Hay was put up in the customary way, with horses, and stacked all around the meadows. In the winter, the stacked hay was loaded on sleds and hauled to a stationary baler. Sometimes the baler was towed out to the hay, but often the baler was kept in a barn and the hay hauled to it. The balers were powered by a steam-engine tractor for years. Later, a gas-driven tractor with a belt drive replaced the steam engine.

At least one all-wooden, water-powered baler was used in a hay barn along the road just south of Leadville, Colorado. The upper Arkansas River was diverted through a canal into the barn and turned a kind of water or Pelton wheel. The plunger ran very slowly but it was also cheap and steady.

Leadville is just under 9,000 feet in elevation, which translates to ten months of winter and two months of poor sledding.

Right across the road from this baler was a railroad that shipped the hay to large cities like Denver and Kansas City. It was always shipped in boxcars to diminish the danger of fire started by the sparks from the engine smoke. It is hard to imagine today, but back then, hay was the petroleum that powered the country. Most of the hay was purchased by Wells Fargo to feed the horses that drew their mail and other delivery wagons around the cities. Much of it also fed the animals that powered the mines.

It normally took one load of hay to deliver one load by horse. This cut the income by half, but $50 per ton but was still enough to operate with a profit. All this meant that the early-day ranchers (more accurately "hay farmers") enjoyed two profit centers: hay and cattle. Even on those high mountain ranches, the cattle were almost never fed hay. Our cattle ranged through the hills to the east, where the snow was shallower, and down onto the prairie just west of Pueblo. In the spring there would be a branding and roundup and the cattle would be drifted back to the mountains for the summer. Thus, they were never fed but grazed out 365 days per year, so their input cost was nil. A bad winter could wipe out most of the herd, and did sometimes, but that was considered a cost of doing business. Hay profits just kept coming.

Later much of this range was homesteaded, curtailing the available range. Following the Taylor Grazing Act of 1934, the Bureau of Land

Management (BLM) was formed in 1946, which meant the end of the ranging and drifting. If a rancher wanted to stay in the cattle business, he had to start feeding hay to his cows instead of selling it. Also at this time the gas engine appeared and hay was replaced by petroleum as the primary fuel. Now there was only one profit center. The cost of raising cattle shot up.

In 1960, I turned 20, and the responsibility for the ranch pretty much came to me. I soon recognized we had a problem. The cost of putting up hay was on the rise but the cattle price was not, and the squeeze began. This forced changes in management to get back to a year-round grazing program. For our ranch—at 7,500 feet, collecting up to three feet of snow on the ground—year-round grazing was a fantasy. Years later, the trucks got big enough to haul the cattle to winter pasture. In those days, however, the trucks were too small to make that feasible. The fact that cows, unaccustomed as they were to the stress of trucking, suffered lower fertility rates as a result, made trucking less attractive.

We often got in excess of 100 inches of snow in the winter, and in the early 1970s, now in my thirties, I got the urge to look for greener pastures.

I went northwest to British Columbia, Canada, several times looking at ranches. The area we liked best was west of Clinton along the Fraser River. That area was famous for its grass: lush enough to finish three- or four-year-old steers! It also was noted for its ability to winter cattle out, and that really intrigued me after the winters we had lived through in Colorado.

The ranch we landed on was the Canoe Creek Ranch, belonging to Jack Koster and his family. The original ranch saddled the Fraser, but when Jack's father died in the '50s, Jack and his brother, Henry, decided to split the property. Jack owned and operated the east half. The half lying on the west side of the river later belonged to a fellow Coloradoan named Bob J.R. Maytag (of the appliance company). In 1974, Bob sold his half, now called Empire Valley, to a German baroness by the name of Sophie Stegeman.

On one of these trips, I was flying to Kamloops and saw Bob Maytag on the same flight. We each talked about what we were doing up there. This was before he had sold to Sophie. After Sophie purchased the ranch, Bob held a fairly large mortgage on it, to be paid in one year

# WE DECIDE TO MOVE

from the proceeds of all the cattle sales. Sophie refused to pay him, so he was forced to take the ranch back. He started that process and, just before he got possession, approached us and suggested we trade. He did not want to try to start his business there again, as his crew had moved back to the States. We said, "No, but call us when the ranch is in your possession." After he took possession he called us, and we met and made the trade. We got the land, some of the machinery, but no cows.

I had visited Empire two times before this. Sophie had wanted me to come on as a partner and bail her out. Of course I wasn't interested. All that to say this: Our exposure to the ranch was so limited that, even at the purchase point, we didn't realize just what we had. We met in Kamloops as arranged by Henry Koster, Jack's brother, a realtor at the time. After the papers were signed, Bob's attorney turned to me and asked, "Just what are you going to do with a 325,000-acre ranch?" With his question, the impact of the decision hit me. I remembered a prayer I had said a few days after Bob came to propose the trade. I had asked the Lord what he wanted me to do, and had sensed his response in a verse from the book of Acts: "Go down and go with them. All is well; I have sent them." Now, and at times since, I wondered about those directions!

The next day I went out to my new ranch and home and was able to hire back some of Maytag's crew to babysit the ranch while I went back to Colorado to pack the family and arrange for the shipping of the purebred cows and our machinery.

Without my fantastic wife, Connie, a childhood sweetheart, this would never have been possible. In all our moves, she has insisted that she not go and see the

Tom and Connie on motorbikes

house but just move into whatever it was and make a home. She got the ultimate test at Empire: the ranch headquarters was 80 miles from the nearest paved road, with no electricity, intermittent phone service, no school, and only the local First Nations people for employees and neighbors.

Connie had been a city girl but loved the mountains and wanted any new place to be very mountainous. When we were looking to buy another ranch, that was one of the requirements she put on the deal. And we both wanted to be at the end of the road.

Another requirement that was important to Connie especially was no rattlesnakes. I'll have more to say about that in a later chapter.

My history with Mrs. Hook goes back to the fourth or fifth grade, when she used to throw rocks at me. I spent my formative years around cows and keenly observed their characteristics. Ever notice how much a heifer is like her mother when she matures?

With this knowledge in hand, I set out to find the perfect girl so I could check out her mother and see whether I could still be married to the daughter when she was the mother's age. When I got into high school, I began to notice this little neighbor girl who looked as if she might be of interest someday. She was in junior high at the time. And her mother sure fit the mold. In my senior year—her freshman year—I decided to approach her and see about the possibilities. She rejected these approaches strongly until, out of frustration, I went back up to the ranch to try to get my mind off the rejection. School was out and I was waiting for graduation. At this time she had a change of heart and, through my brother, sent a nice blue shirt to me with a note to give her a call. Within seconds, I was on the phone with her and we set up our first date.

We wouldn't marry for seven years. We both completed college, and I also did a stint in the Air Force. All this time my folks were against the relationship, as they thought she was too silly and too pretty for me. (Connie sometimes didn't help, like the time she asked my dad, "Mr. Hook, do horses give milk?") I knew she would grow out of the silliness, and the other was no problem for me. Finally, the day came when my mother called me in and said they would give their approval to our marriage.

We were married June 6, 1964. Ever since that day, she has been right there under my arm, where she belongs.

# WE DECIDE TO MOVE

Tom and Connie Hook

Her perspective on this move is an important part of the story. You need to hear what she has to say.

## His Calling

I awoke early and looked around. Then I remembered: we were in the guest room of our dear friends and neighbors, Jim and Connie (see p.140). Everything came back to me: "Well, this is it! A new beginning for my husband, our two small sons, and myself." As I rolled over, I looked at my husband, who was lying awake staring at the ceiling, deep in thought about the future ahead. I wanted to just snuggle into his arms and have him reassure me that we were doing the right thing, but I felt he needed this time alone with his thoughts to plan our next few hours.

I closed my eyes and pictured my own home, just three miles down the road. Tom's family had lived there for 100 years. Now the rooms were empty, the walls and cupboards bare, and the curtains that make a home cozy gone. Could I go back to that house this morning and say goodbye to the home that had given us so many happy memories?

Our son's first steps, the kitchen where so many birthday cakes had been baked and decorated, the warm fireplace where we spent our cold winter evenings, discussing the day's activities or making new plans.

My stomach had an empty feeling I was sure my breakfast could not fill. As I felt Tom turn over, I knew this day would be even harder for him. That empty house had been his home since he was a newborn, when his father and mother brought him home from the hospital. Tom's parents, grandparents and great-grandparents had ranched in this beautiful high mountain valley of Colorado. He was the fourth generation on that ranch. Today, that heritage would end.

The smell of fresh-perked coffee began to filter into our room from Connie's kitchen. It was time to get up and face the day. As Tom and I knelt in prayer, all we could ask our Lord for was courage. Only then could we face the day with a new strength.

After a good breakfast and a hard goodbye to our friends, who had opened their home for our last night in this beautiful valley, we headed down the road to our final drive into the lane we had entered so many years. The semi-truck faced the road, loaded with all our furniture and personal belongings. The corrals looked quiet without the animals we had fed each morning in our routine chores. As I entered the house, the emptiness seemed to close in on me, and I felt a chill go down my back. Our boys ran through the house, their squeals echoing off the bare walls. They were so small. I wondered if they fully understood that this was no longer their home.

I sat down on the rug in the middle of our living room floor and they came running to me with outstretched arms, happy that I was sitting down to play. As I held them in my arms, God reminded me that as these boys fully put their trust in Tom and me, so I must also trust God with the dependent faith of a small child. No questions asked, just trust.

I made one last pass through the house to make sure we hadn't left anything. I heard a car pull into the driveway and looked out to see Tom's parents and my own parents getting out. They had come to say goodbye and help with any last-minute packing. My heart went out to Tom's parents as I saw them look at the mountains with their snow-capped peaks, the valley floor, and the land they had worked for so many years. I knew this was a very hard day for them. They had retired, yet they also were saying goodbye to a way of life they had always known.

# WE DECIDE TO MOVE

Colorado ranch

As Tom's mother entered the house, I saw in her eyes a sadness she was trying to hide. I put my arms around her and, in the silence, we seemed to know each other's struggles. Like Tom, she had grown up in this house, and had many memories racing through her mind.

The driver started the semi. As it warmed up, we stood by the car, hugging and saying goodbye. I felt the strength and courage we had prayed for earlier. We started out the driveway, and I took one last look at the ranch and the house we had loved so much. Why must we leave? Why could we not get rid of the desire and drive that kept calling us? We could be so happy here. Our small boys would soon be ready to start school, and the schools here were so good! Why must we leave our families who stood in the road waving goodbye? Why? Why?

Then that small voice inside me said, "Because I, your Lord God, have called you to carry my Word to a remote area in British Columbia, Canada."

I turned the car onto the highway, behind Tom in our pickup, and we headed north to a new country, new people, a new ranch, and a new beginning. The tears were now coming freely. I had held them back, but now they finally came. Tears of sadness, yes, but tears of excitement as well.

For three days, we followed Tom north. As we passed ranching and farming communities, I wondered if these families had followed a calling to move to this land—or were they the third or fourth generation on that farm?

Many times, my mind drifted to the ranch we had bought in the remote and isolated area of British Columbia. I had never been on our new ranch or seen the house that I was to make into our new home. I wondered if I would be able to understand the life and ways of the Native people who made up the sparse population of the area and would be our ranch workers.

However, my biggest concern was the long distance from the ranch to town, making it impossible for our boys to attend a school. When the time came, our home would have to serve as our school. Fear hit again! But again, the fear was overcome by the overwhelming power of God's presence.

The morning of the fourth day, I again awoke in a strange bed, this time in a motel in Clinton, B.C., the last town I was to see for quite

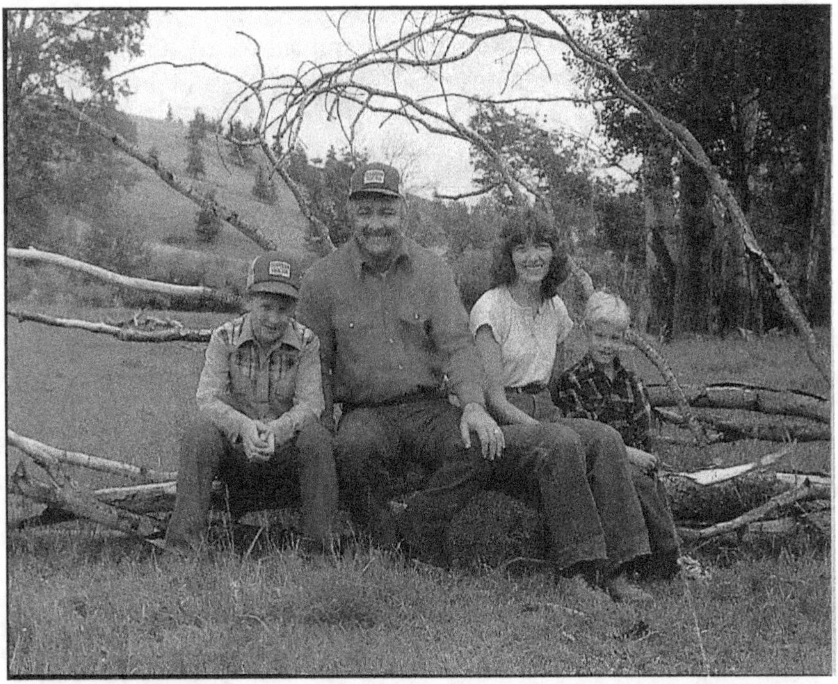

Hook family at Empire

KAMLOOPS DAILY SENTINEL

VOL. 98
NO. 165
18 PAGES

The Home Newspaper for Kamloops and South Central British Columbia

KAMLOOPS, BRITISH COLUMBIA, SATURDAY, JULY 16, 1977

SINGLE COPY 20¢
HOME DELIVERY 85¢ PER WEEK

TOM AND CONNIE HOOK, from Colorado are the new owners of the Empire Valley Ranch, 75 miles west of Clinton. They have four horses, two dogs and 50 head of cattle. Hook said he is giving the land a rest before he purchases some registered cattle. The Hooks look on ranching as exciting and don't mind the isolation. Shown here is their oldest child Therron, four years old.

Beverley Dalton Photo

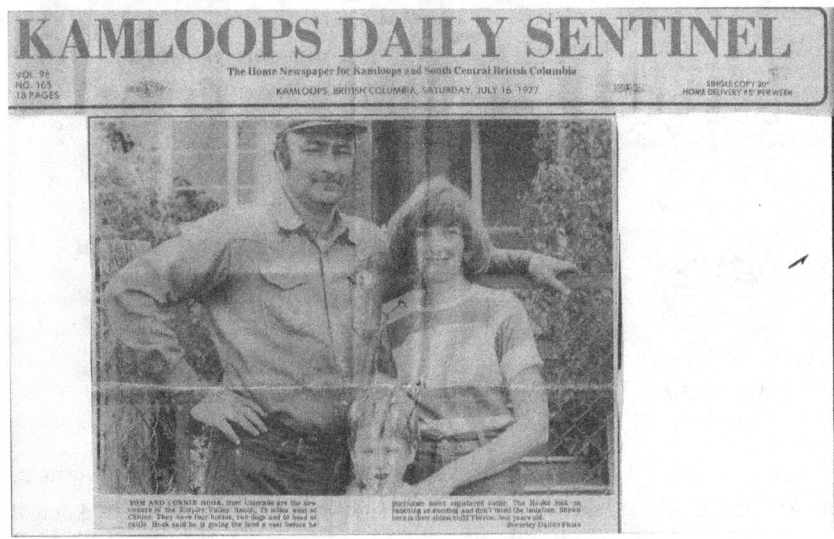

Article in Kamloops, BC paper featuring Hook family purchase of Empire Valley

some time. But now I was even happier and felt secure having Tom by my side. God had given me this man as my provider and protector, and He also gave Tom the ability to sense when I needed comforting most. Again, the butterflies were fluttering in my stomach; today we would arrive at our new ranch and new life. I felt Tom's arms pull me close, and I closed my eyes and thanked God, once again, for this man.

After hurriedly shopping through the small grocery store, trying to think of everything I would need to set up a kitchen for a month, we were finally ready for the last leg of our long journey. My precious mother had accompanied us on the trip, to help me drive and care for our boys. I looked over at her face, weary but strong. I knew I could never have made this trip without her. God knew that, also, and had used her in many ways to give me the strength and courage I needed along the way.

Road to Clinton

A few miles north of town we turned off the smooth pavement to be greeted by a bumpy dirt road. With excitement in my heart, I felt it won't be long now, and I will be seeing my new home. Even though Tom had warned me of the distance from this small town, my excitement had shortened the road considerably in my mind. After an hour of bumping along the dusty, dirty road, my spirits began to sink again. My mother saw my shoulders droop and said, "Surely we will soon be there!"

Road to Clinton

Another hour went by, and again my mother looked my way. I knew what she was thinking: "How will my daughter ever be able to take this rough and rugged life out here, so far from town?"

Tom pulled over and stopped. He must have guessed how anxious I was getting. He reassured me we were almost at our new home. In fact, we were now on our ranch! Wow, we were finally on our land now, starting into our new driveway. Now it would be only minutes until I would be seeing our new home for the first time.

Ten minutes went by, then 15, 20 … . My hands shook as I steered the car in and out of the sharp, winding corners of the narrow little road high above the Fraser River below. Finally, 45 minutes after Tom said we were on our ranch, we topped a hill and saw, in the valley below, the ranch headquarters awaiting us.

Alfalfa fields stretched up the sides of the mountains. I saw an old barn that could probably tell many a story. I saw the Russell fences that made up the corrals. They were empty, but soon we would be filling them with our own cattle. The sight of it all was awesome. The place was plenty rundown, but it was beautiful to my wondering eyes.

Empire Valley headquarters

As we dropped down a small hill, crossed the tiny creek, and topped the next hill, there stood our house, the sight I had been longing to see for so long. It was simple … but beautiful.

Hook family home at Empire

# WE DECIDE TO MOVE

As Tom and I walked up the sidewalk to the front door, I felt my legs become like lead weights. Would I be disappointed and, if so, would I be able to hide it from Tom, who at this point was bubbling over with excitement?

As we stepped into the empty house with bare walls and windows, my mind went back to the clean house I had left behind. I looked down at the soiled rug. A dirty mattress lay in the middle of the floor. A musty smell struck my nose. We walked into the kitchen; a wall was black from an old fire. I tentatively peeked into the cupboards, one by one. When I opened the doors under the sink and saw maggots, the tears I was trying to fight rose to sting my eyes. Yet Tom's reassuring, strong arm was around me, and I could feel the Lord's presence. It was my mother who spoke in her hopeful way: "This place has real possibility!"

After touring the rest of the house, I caught Mom's optimism, and began to see my new home through fresh eyes. I could envision clean floors and shining windows fitted with clean, crisp curtains and new plant starts on the windowsills. I could almost smell bread baking in the woodstove.

We stood in the mess and thanked God for the new hopes and promises we could see ahead. We thanked Him for the vision to look ahead, to see beyond the problems into a beautiful future.

Second newspaper article with his and hers perspectives

Yes, there would be more problems, but not without God's promise to carry us, His children, into that "promised land" of milk and honey. To Him be the glory!

# CHAPTER TWO

# BIG MOVE TO A BIG RANCH

My family and I, several friends, and two dogs drove 1,684 miles to Empire Valley. It took us three days to reach the ranch and another two to move in. We had to buy enough groceries to last a couple of weeks, as the ranch was 80 miles and three hours from the closest town. We had wanted to get away from subdivisions and ski areas; I guess we really outdid ourselves.

Fraser River with Empire in background

# BIG MOVE TO A BIG RANCH

Before leaving Colorado, I got a call from the man I had hired to watch the ranch. He said the upper two irrigation storage lakes had washed out, leaving just the lowest one, Brown's Lake, holding all the water. This meant only the lower half of the fields would get irrigation water. At that point I decided not to put any cattle on the ranch for the first year, because we weren't expecting to have much hay the next winter.

Actually, another unforeseen development interfered with the move of the cattle. I had planned to take all the heifers from our commercial herd, which we had bred continually from 1906 to 1977. However they reacted to their Bangs vaccination and had to be sold in Colorado.

The purebred cows, and the machinery, did get delivered during the first summer. But not without some interesting (to put it mildly) complications.

Registered cattle at Colorado ranch

The purebreds had to be tested for blue tongue before they were ready to travel. Steve Oswald, our manager in Colorado, started this process. He had the blood drawn for the test and shipped to the lab in Denver. The lab informed him that it had not received the blood in time and could not test it. By now we were running out of time on our immigration permit. So he ran everything through again and this time personally delivered the blood to the lab and waited for the results. With the report in hand, he raced home to load the cattle. We had only hours to get them across the border. He loaded the cattle and they left for B.C. They were to cross the border at Oroville, Washington, and get unloaded in Okanagan Falls, B.C.

When they were supposed to have arrived, I called the sale yard in Okanagan Falls, but they had no cattle for me and weren't expecting any. This meant we had a load of purebred cattle, and a couple of horses, lost somewhere in the Northwest without a trace and no way to call to find them. I almost went into panic mode because the clock was still ticking. I called the trucker we had hired to pick them up from the Canadian side, and he came up with the bright idea that they just might be at the sale yards in Okanagan, Washington, on the other side of the border, instead of Okanagan Falls, B.C.. I called the barn in Okanagan and they said, yes, they did have a load of cattle for me. The trucker from B.C. left immediately for the six-hour trip down and got back and crossed the border with literally minutes to spare. The next day, he delivered the cattle and horses to Empire.

But there was another small hurdle we had to clear. Trucks could not get into the ranch headquarters at Empire Valley. The limiting factor, besides the narrow winding road, was a weight restriction for the suspension bridge across the Fraser River. We would have to use horses to push the cattle across the bridge and then all the way down our 18-mile lane.

There was a heavy skid-mounted loading chute at the bridge, so we positioned it so the truck could back onto the bridge just far enough to use the chute. That way, the cattle came off the truck already started across the bridge, and we were saved the almost impossible task of trying to get them to step onto a swinging suspension bridge a quarter-mile long.

My wife volunteered to trail the cattle home. She was assisted by a (not very competent) employee. After riding on the trucks for several days, these animals had to walk the last 18 miles. I always felt rather bad about their introduction to their new home. We put them out on our best close-in pastures, and somehow they seemed to forget and forgive.

Empire Valley Ranch had no boundary fences. Rather, natural barriers like Churn Creek served that purpose.

Churn Creek

This unscalable creek separated us from the Gang Ranch for 76 miles, the length of both our ranges.

You could ride a horse from one end of Empire to the other in a day if you started before daylight, changed horses at noon and ended about dark. I know this because our older son rode this trip in one day at the age of 14. He had started going to the mountains with the Native cowboys at the age of 12, much to his mother's chagrin. He is without a doubt the most natural and gifted horseman and cowman I have ever known; he never knew anything else.

**Young Theron mounted in Empire back country**

All our present neighbors rely on his rope and cattle abilities. He is a keen appraiser of the condition of our range cows and tells me "they are happy or PO'd."

There were no roads from the headquarters into our summer range in the Coast Mountains; when you left the barn you saddled up in the spring and returned in the fall. To supply the cow camps with food and hay was a drive of 265 miles one way. I had to go back out to the major highway and then around through Lillooett and along Bridge Lake

Moving cattle to Empire summer range

to get to the Relay Creek cow camp. My family and I lived many summers at that camp with the Native cowboys and a bunch of horses and dogs. We were usually there from July 1st through September 1st. This range was called Tyaughton, "good little things from the ground" in the Shuswap language. The legend was that early winter snows trapped a group of Natives in that valley and they survived on rock chucks (yellow-bellied marmots), a variety of ground squirrel.

Empire was miles beyond the nearest utility service, so one of our very first projects would be the installation of a hydro-powered electricity generator (see Appendix C). Maytag had commissioned a feasibility study for hydropower and was told it wasn't possible. But it looked to me like there was sufficient water if I could get enough drop in elevation to produce the power and speed we needed. In the meantime, the ranch had an old Caterpillar generator that used about a gallon of oil a day. We ran it only for an hour each morning and evening to keep the fridges and freezers cold.

Empire hydro power plant

The next chapter in our Empire story could be very negative because of the woman from whom Maytag had repossessed the ranch. She probably figured she had a reason to hate us.

Back in 1974, after Sophie had purchased the ranch from Bob Maytag, she was moving all her things from Germany to Canada. In Germany, she and her children were very big into raising Hanoverian Jumpers.

These animals, big enough to resemble workhorses, were fairly rare. Sophie wanted to bring several to Empire so they could continue breeding. She went down to Vancouver and hired a 737 cargo plane to fly to Wiesbaden, Germany, to bring back the horses. When the plane arrived in Germany the government would not allow the release of the horses, so the plane returned home empty. She demanded that they turn around and go back, this time with her on board. This time they got the horses loaded but couldn't get cleared for takeoff. They sat on the runway for eight hours waiting for authorization. Apparently, she owed back taxes and the government was holding the only assets they could.

Meanwhile, the sedative on the horses was wearing off. Finally, the clearance came and they flew back to Vancouver. I have no idea what that fiasco cost.

When Sophie departed Empire she left some cattle behind. They had taken the rest out to Kamloops but apparently couldn't gather the last 52 head. I came across them grazing near a set of corrals about five miles above the house. My wife and I were able to haze them into the corral. We went home and sent two cowboys to go back up and bring them home.

When I had the cattle in the corrals at the house I called Sophie and told her. She said "Oh no, you MUST turn them back out and I will come get them before the snow." This was in July. I told her that was not acceptable and I would call the trucker and have him haul the cattle to the sale yard in Kamloops, sell them, and have the check, minus the freight, mailed to her. She yelled for several minutes at me but I called the trucker anyway. The cattle left, and I think she intercepted them and paid the freight.

Another time a very agitated man called me from north of Kamloops.

"Is this Empire Valley?" he asked. I answered in the affirmative.

"What are you going to do about these cows?" Not following him, I asked what cows he was talking about.

# BIG MOVE TO A BIG RANCH

"The cows that fell in the river in the winter and got dragged out onto my property, and I want you to come and do something about them."

At this point I got very interested. We bordered the Fraser River and had just purchased a large herd of cows and moved them onto the ranch. Might we have lost some?

"Just where are you and the cows located?" I asked him.

"On the Thompson River north of Kamloops."

That was 200 miles east of us and on an entirely different river. To get there, our cows would have had to float down the river for 100 miles in the Fraser River and then float up the Thompson about the same distance. The physics seemed pretty straightforward, but I had the hardest time trying to explain to him that this was not possible. In the end he accepted the fact and resigned himself to his fate. I told him that after working with Sophie for several years the smartest thing he could do was to just bury those cows and forget about Sophie. The grief she would have given him would not have been worth the hassle.

Sometime later, I heard that Sophie had had several cows break through the ice, drown, and float away near Little Fort.

I have a friend who also moved to Canada and operated a big, remote ranch in mountain country in British Columbia. His experience was virtually identical to mine, except he worked as a manager instead of an owner-operator. Anyway, he told me that he wouldn't take $10 million for his experiences, but he wouldn't pay 10 cents to do it again. I guess it has to do with age.

Now that my boys can run things and have good wives who can take it, leaving me to just sit around and complain, I would go back there in a heartbeat.

When my time comes, I wouldn't mind dying on the banks of the Fraser in some of God's most beautiful country. The locals say that anyone who ever drinks from the Fraser River will come back. We both drank there and made our kids do it, too. Pretty muddy.

Tom sheep hunting on Fraser benchlands, Empire

# CHAPTER THREE

# LIFE AT EMPIRE

The road into Empire crosses Churn Creek, the border between Gang and Empire. From there it runs about 15 miles to the headquarters and gains about 1,500 feet in elevation.

Churn Creek canyon

Churn Creek canyon runs 30 miles westward and made an excellent border "fence." It is deep and rough, and cattle almost never crossed it.

## LIFE AT EMPIRE

Along that distance there were only about three places that had narrow trails down from the plateaus on each side where animals could cross. Occasionally one would manage it, but very rarely.

Churn Creek grassland, Gang Ranch in background

The Churn Creek grasslands were an integral part of Empire Valley Ranch. The government of B.C. has now purchased Empire Valley and declared this part a Provincial Grassland, having chosen this site because of what they said were its "pristine" qualities. A grassland like this is still pristine after 150 years of annual grazing. We used this pasture for November and December grazing every year we were there. Two years, we were able to leave our cows on this range until mid-February.

About eight miles up this canyon was a small gold mine claim that two miners were working during the summer. The miners lived a cabin on the claim. I don't think they worked very hard at the gold digging or panning but mostly used this place as a summer getaway. At the cabin they kept a scantily clad, life-sized inflatable Playboy Bunny. When they returned to civilization in the winter they left the bunny at the cabin; that was probably the right decision since they had wives back home.

The bunny seemed to fascinate some of the cowboys, and they often rode down to see if she was still in residence. On one of those outings two Native cowboys arrived at the cabin to find the miners there. The miners invited the two in for coffee, and they happily consented. When they walked in, the bunny was standing in the corner of the kitchen looking at them. One of these Native cowboys was very much into indigenous religious practices and Spiritism. They had just started enjoying the fresh coffee when this fellow leaped up from his chair, ran out the door, jumped on his horse and "gave 'er both sides" up the trail toward home.

The other cowboy visited while enjoying his coffee and then leisurely left back up the trail. When he reached the top, he found his companion sitting on his horse, looking back down at the cabin. He asked him why he had left in such a rude hurry. "She winked at me," was his reply. To my knowledge, he never went near there again.

The last we heard, the bunny was hanging in a tree along the trail. Probably put there by one of the miner's wives when she discovered who her husband was spending his summers with.

The neighborhood post office was at the Gang Ranch, our nearest neighbor, 45 minutes north on a 15-mile gravel road. The mail stage, as it was called, delivered the mail once a week, to our mailbox at the end of the lane, 12 miles from the house, where the road forked off to Gang Ranch. We met them at noon every Wednesday, as they also brought any groceries we had ordered. In addition, they always checked at the bus depot in town for any shipments. That's how we got all our vaccine and vet supplies shipped from Province Livestock Supply in Lethbridge, Alberta.

For a while, the postmistress at the Gang Ranch post office was a Native lady who couldn't read or write. She just spread all the mail out on a large table and told everybody to take what was theirs and leave the rest alone. This story actually made the Reader's Digest. She eventually absconded with the petty cash, moved back across the river to the local

## LIFE AT EMPIRE

reserve, and changed her name. I believe the theft involved a total of $132.84, not to mention the fact that it was a federal offense.

One of the complexities of life at Empire, given its remoteness, was the limited education opportunities for the kids. Our boys, Theron and Tristan, were schooled at the kitchen table until we acquired some real desks.

The nearest public school was at Gang Ranch. This option would have required my wife to make four trips a day over that road—not a welcome prospect, especially in winter conditions. Empire had had a school the year before we arrived, but we were short of the minimum seven students. (A former owner of Empire once advertised in the Vancouver Sun for an employee "with seven kids, work skills negotiable.") When we arrived, a portable school building was still at the headquarters, but the school board moved it to Gang Ranch when they learned we weren't going to use it. (That move was quite a chore, as the truckers had to back the trailer around most of the narrow switchbacks on our road.)

The nice thing about home schooling was that, while a trip to town took several days, the kids could go along and keep up with their schoolwork. Longer family trips with a motor home were also possible. To top it off, the boys could hunt, fish, ride,

Theron and Tristan home schooling

A mounted Tristan Hook at Empire Valley

or rope after school every day instead of riding on a bus. No homework was also a plus, at least for them. And while we were constantly being criticized for their lack of exposure to peers, we saw this as a big advantage. We have never regretted that they were only around adults while growing up. Their friends were all adult First Nations people.

Theron with Alec and George Rosette

These cowboys certainly had their effect on the boys. It was all basically good, but our older son got awfully tired of listening to the marital problems of the cowboys for the millionth time.

Sometimes we wondered if our boys might lack some social skills because of their isolation at Empire. But twelve years later, when we moved to Oregon, they finished in public school. Both were salutatorians of their respective classes (even though Theron spent his entire senior year playing poker). Tristan was president of the student body and a state FFA officer and traveled for a year with that organization.

In his senior year he built a gooseneck trailer in shop class. So the years at Empire didn't seem to hurt them.

The nearest doctor was two hours away in Clinton. (The sign on the front of his small office building read "Hickory Dickory Doc.") Theron was kicked in the ribs one time and suffered bruises on several internal organs. The horse was sharp-shod so the wounds went pretty deep. We had deep snow and had to call for an airplane to land at Gang Ranch to fly him to the hospital in Williams Lake.

The doctor in Clinton was pretty good. One day he looked into one of our boys' ears and saw a small, round, shiny object. It turned out to be a gum-wrapper spitball. Of course we wanted to know the story. He said some other kids had told him if he put it in one ear and then cocked his head it would fall through. The sobering part of that story was that we hadn't lived near those kids for about five years!

The Natives had the same health care and schooling opportunities, except that they usually moved to the reserve during the school year, where there were more than seven kids.

Soon after we arrived at Empire we realized that we weren't actually at the end of the road after all; a hippie had a cabin five miles farther. The cabin was located along Lone Cabin Creek, very appropriately named. Actually, there was no road to the cabin, only a narrow trail that passed the cabin, crossed the creek, and went south along the river.

The trail was along a very steep hillside that dropped straight off for several hundred feet into Lone Cabin Creek. In the early days it had been used as the main transportation link between Vancouver and the gold mines in the upper Interior. In the winter, the pack strings would stop and winter their horses on a flat-topped mountain near the house at Empire. That mountain rarely had snow too deep for a horse to paw through. The only exception was a silver thaw: winter rain on snow, followed by a hard freeze that caused crusting. If such a rain came on top of a foot or more of snow, the horses couldn't paw through it. They would have to be brought in and fed hay or moved to pastures where the sun had melted the ice crust. Whenever we rode up there, we had to protect our horses' front legs. We made leggings by cutting an inner tube to the proper length and slipping it over the horse's leg. A piece of twine over the horse's shoulder held the leggings up, while another twine running down and in a groove through the shoes held it down. This arrangement worked very well.

Of course, the pack trains were long gone when we were at Empire, but we wintered pack strings for several hunting guides. These guides were some of the finest men we worked with in B.C. After wintering these horses for years, we got a feel for the history of the area. [1]

Our hippie neighbor told me that one winter a silver thaw came in while he was at the cabin. Everything was covered with ice, and he had to crawl nearly four miles to get to the basket that crossed the river so he could go to town.

Most winters this loner hippie worked for a local ranch. Usually he stayed down at the Gang pasture along the river. About two o'clock one morning, a car raced through our yard and headed out along the road (more a trail, really) to his cabin. I usually didn't allow anybody in there, so I was a bit surprised at their brazenness. Far too sleepy to give chase, I decided to wait until daylight before investigating. In a couple of hours the car came back through and headed out the main road. It was an older Volvo that I didn't recognize.

The next day the hippie came into the headquarters, looking rather poorly, and wanted us to take him to town to a doctor. He had been at a party at his girlfriend's house across the river. Everybody got high on happy weed, a fight broke out, and he broke up all their musical instruments. At this, they beat him up and decided to put him in the trunk of the car, take him down to the suspension bridge, and throw him in the Fraser River to drown. They were in the middle of the bridge ready to throw him over the rail when some Natives came along, so they had to put him back in the trunk. They decided to take him home through our yard. After they got him near enough to his house that he could walk the rest of the way, they beat him up again, hit his head against the car until one of his eardrums was broken, removed his pants, and left him lying at the end of the road. They also took all his guns except for a .22 rifle.

Another time, when I was working in the field below the house, a man came walking from the direction of the lone cabin. It was a hot

---

[1] One particular piece of history we did not experience. Apparently some packer got the bright idea of using camels instead of horses. One can only imagine how all hell must have broken loose when a camel came up on a string of pack horses.

day, but he was holding a light jacket against his throat. He walked up to the house and asked my wife to sew up his throat. It had a hole about an inch wide and three inches long; you could see all the veins and the trachea. Connie did not want to tackle a repair job so close to major blood vessels. They summoned me to ask if I would attempt to repair the wound. I had had lots of experience sewing up cows, but I declined and suggested they head to town for a doctor. He refused, offering no explanation. We disinfected the wound and he went down to the bunkhouse to wait for the hippie to come in from work. Later, the hippie came up to the house and explained that his friend did not want to go to town because he had jumped bail and was being sought by the RCMP. [2]

Later that night they decided to take a chance and head to town, but they needed to borrow a pickup. I gave them the use of a small Scout pickup and they headed out about 9 p.m. The next day I got a call that the pickup had been stolen in town and then found, but the motor was no longer working. Later that day, a friend of ours hauled the two out to Dog Creek to meet me to take them back to Empire. When they got out of the car, everyone—my friend and his wife, the hippie and his buddy—was covered with dust. The driver was new to these roads and left his windows partway down, hoping to push a breeze through the car, but the effect was simply to suck the dust in. I think after that he kept his windows rolled up.

We took a truck into town and hauled the Scout back to Empire. Crazy Ron, the friend of the injured man, said the engine damage was his fault and he wanted to stay around long enough to repair it. He pulled the engine out, and I took it back into town to be rebuilt. While that was happening, a range specialist from the forestry department came to visit for a weekend. He heard the story and thought he should report Crazy Ron's whereabouts to the RCMP, which he did. Crazy Ron found out about it and ran away into the mountains to hide. He said later that every time a small plane went over he was sure it was looking for him, and it bothered him so much he came back to the headquarters to give himself up.

But before he turned himself in, the RCMP called me. They said they knew where he was, and would we mind keeping him until his trial

---

[2] Royal Canadian Mounted Police

date, coming up in a couple of months? They said he had been so obnoxious while they were holding him they just wanted to be rid of him. I finally agreed, and he stayed around and worked for us. Later, I found out that he had been charged with attempted murder. He had forced two Korean men out of their Chevy Blazer and then drove it over a cliff, leaving them to walk 30 miles back to town in their street clothes. It was 30 degrees below zero at the time and they developed terrible frostbite and nearly died from exposure.

Another time, the hippie stopped in our yard with a billy goat in the back of his truck. That billy stunk so bad our yard reeked for several hours after they left. It's hard to describe how terrible that goat smelled. The next day I was in the area above his cabin where he had parked his truck and found the goat, dead beside his truck. Maybe the billy smelled of death as well as essence of goat.

As for the girlfriend, she eventually became his wife. She was a very attractive, French-speaking girl who liked to ride horseback. She would come over to our house to buy cream (Connie and our foreman's wife, Nancy, milked a cow and always had extra cream). She would put the cream in a jar, tie it behind her saddle, and head home. The action of the horse would churn the cream, and by the time she had traveled the five miles home, she had butter. They also ate a lot of nettle. Connie always really liked this girl and respected her.

For years I have worn Eddie Bauer caps, a flannel affair with side flaps that come down to cover your ears. My wife swears I'd wear my hat, complete with ear flaps, in July if a cloud came over. That is probably right, as I froze my ears hunting cougars when I was very young and, ever since, my ears have been very sensitive to the cold.

One time while we were living in Canada we flew to Denver for the stock show. My hat was getting just a little

Connie with Gary Brumbelow modeling Tom's infamous hat

# LIFE AT EMPIRE

dirty and worn-out, so we went to the Eddie Bauer store in downtown Denver to try to find a replacement. I had to drag my wife along, complaining all the way. She had envisioned the day my old hat would die and I would be forced to change styles. I looked around the store and couldn't find the hat I wanted, so I asked the manager. He said that model was out of production. My heart sank—and I could have sworn my wife was jumping up and down on the inside and silently squealing with joy at the prospect of finally being rid of that hat. But she was crestfallen when the manager said he still had some in storage in the basement.

We went to the basement and, sure enough, there they were! He had nine, so I bought them all. My wife nearly fainted. I now had a lifetime supply. Not until we were back home did we discover why they were in storage: the bill was sewn on a little crooked. This strange look mortified my wife even more. Even today, if I want to rattle her chain I just put on my "EDDIE BAUER" hat.

Our family jokes about my numerous, and sometimes even successful, bright ideas. One "bright idea" I came up with before we moved to B.C. was to get my pilot's license. The flying experiences were more white-knuckle than humorous, but they tended to make lasting memories. Given the size of the operation at Empire, and the extreme terrain, I was convinced it would be very helpful to have the option of aerial inspection of the ranch in general and the cattle in particular.

I wanted to be ready to go before arriving at Empire, so I started training in a small mountain town near our ranch in Colorado. The landing strip was especially tricky, as it sloped steeply from end to end, was situated at a very high altitude, and had no alternative runway to use when the crosswinds were bad. This meant that you had only one direction for takeoff and landing, no matter which way the wind was blowing. Given this reality, I landed more than once with very white knuckles and a heart rate higher than I care to remember.

After I finished the course we decided we needed a plane, so we bought a local Skylane 182. Since the pilot's license and the plane were acquired for the purpose of spotting cattle, we thought we should try the plane out. We quickly found that the plane could not be flown at speeds slow enough to see the animals below with any detail. So we sold that plane and began looking for one more suitable to our purpose.[3]

Shortly after we sold the first plane, we started into the deal with Bob Maytag to buy Empire. Bob was a great pilot and flew almost everywhere he went. We needed to make several trips to B.C. to work out the details. He insisted that we fly together in his twin-engine Baron, which was fast and comfortable for the long flights. After we started our travels, he took delivery on a new plane that he had specifically picked out for Empire because of its flight characteristics, before he had ever thought of selling the ranch. This plane was a Helio Courier.

A Helio was especially suited to our purposes, given its remarkable handling capabilities. It can take off and land from a tennis court, can remain airborne at 28 mph, and can be nosed up and turned around virtually on its tail. This last ability was especially useful to avoid getting trapped in one of the narrow valleys that are so characteristic of mountain country. In such a box canyon any other plane would crash, but the Helio allowed you to turn around in an unbelievably small space and fly back the way you came in.

When we went up for a demonstration ride in the Helio we eventually purchased, we flew out over the ocean a short distance when the pilot spotted a small fishing ship. When he was right over it, he said, "Watch that ship and see where it is after we turn around." He then gave the plane full throttle and pointed it straight up and then moved the yoke to turn. We did two 360s, right over the ship the whole time.

Tom's Helio Courier. His interpretation of the registration number" "See, God is my resource!"

---

[3] Speaking of using fast planes to view cattle, I had a friend who owned a commercial charter service that only flew a very fast twin-engine aircraft. Among his regular customers were the founders of Superior Auction. After chartering his services for several long trips, they hired him to take them up with a camera so they could film their cattle. But given the speed of the plane, the longest film they made was about 3 seconds and very blurry. So I wasn't the only one who had to scrap a bright idea.

Although in 15 years of flying I never had occasion to use that maneuver, it was good to know it was there if I needed it.

Empire had two landing strips. The better one was on a flat-top mountain about eight miles from the house, up a pretty bad road. This strip was approachable from either direction, so you could always land or take off into the wind. The only problem was that it ended at the edge of a cliff; the ground dropped away very fast after takeoff. The effect was pretty dramatic, especially for inexperienced passengers. They often would try to stand up in the plane and sometimes didn't get over the shock until we were back on good old Mother Earth again.

The road to that strip was impassable in the winter, so the other strip had to be used much of the time. This strip was in a hay field right below the headquarters. It was accessible year-round and was just a few hundred feet from the house. But it had a major downside. Landing on this strip was something like landing in a giant bathtub. You had to drop quickly and touch down at the bottom of a steeply sloping meadow. If you missed the landing, you faced the end of the tub, hoping you could climb fast enough to avoid the surrounding mountains.

Empire Valley Ranch was the monster you couldn't tame. If you ever let your guard down for a second, it got you. As in, when all the lakes washed out while I was in Colorado packing.

The first summer was the most challenging, even though we didn't have any cattle until the purebreds arrived.

In June we had our D8 Caterpillar trucked up from Colorado. Of course it got lost, too, but after a week or so it showed up at the B.C. border. Hauling it required a three-axle trailer, not legal in Canada at the time. So the Cat had to be unloaded at the border, walked across, and then reloaded on a trailer legal in Canada. The blade had been detached and was lying on the truck, so it had to be dragged by the Cat or hoisted onto another truck. We sent a crane truck that could pick up the blade and haul it to Kamloops. In the meantime, another truck loaded the Cat and headed for Empire. That trucker got lost on a logging road behind Gang Ranch and tore the rear end out of his truck on a steep section of the road. He radioed in and they sent another truck, which went to the site, picked up the trailer and Cat, and proceeded toward Empire. This time they insisted that I meet the truck and lead him in. Near the

Gang Ranch headquarters was a small bridge that we couldn't cross with either the truck or the Cat. So we unloaded the Cat and walked it in the last twenty miles.

When we finally got the Cat we immediately started rebuilding the washed-out lakes. We also began another gigantic project: installing our "impossible" hydro turbine. I say "impossible" because Bob Maytag had hired a consulting firm to analyze our site, which concluded it wasn't feasible. I wasn't convinced and didn't know better than to just try.

We didn't get any help on the design or installation. I measured the water flow with a homemade plywood weir and used common surveying equipment to measure the fall. I had never used surveying equipment before, but through trial and error we estimated the fall. (After the system was operating, the psi figures indicated that our estimations of fall had been very close.)

Since we had to survey down a very steep hill with lots of downed timber, we used a 40-foot hand line section to sight from, and then just counted the number of times we had to move down the hill. Twelve times meant 480 feet, which turned out to be right on. That hill was so steep we had to pull the welder up the hill with a Cat to weld the steel pipe.

I ordered the Pelton wheel and the generator from a company in Washington and started cutting the road to lay the pipe. I figured we needed all the drop we could get, which required traversing some very rugged country. The route for the pipe ran around a particularly steep and dangerous hillside and then dropped straight down a very steep grade into the yard below

Flyer for the hydro generator

the house. The installed pipe was 10 inches by 4,000 feet long, with 484 feet of fall. This yielded 165 pounds of pressure at 165 feet per second. If you directed this stream at a car it would literally peel the paint off.

We went to Seattle to buy a welder and came back and started the installation. For about 2,000 feet, the route was so steep and sandy we had to use a small Cat to drag a truck with the welder in the back.

It was late in the fall when we finished and I started covering the pipe with dirt. But before I could finish, it turned cold and the pipe froze. Only one short section was exposed. It thawed in a few days and we got to try our new generator. What a difference from the old diesel plant! The hydro was quiet, free, and worked great. We did find when it turned really cold and the creeks froze up high there wasn't enough water to generate power, so for several weeks every winter we had to revert to the diesel plant. By this time, we had traded the Cat power plant for a smaller Lister. We used the Lister as backup the whole time we were there.

The worst problem for the hydro was the debris that plugged the inlet screen. In the summer it was leaves; in the winter, floating ice. But all in all it worked very well. The nozzle had an inside diameter of 15/16 inch. The water was at a pressure of nearly 200 psi when it entered the nozzle. A shaft right at the outlet of the nozzle could be adjusted to either deflect the water off the wheel for less power or directly onto the wheel for full power. A Woodward governor sensed the speed of the wheel and adjusted the deflection of the water stream to keep a constant rpm and subsequently a steady current for power to the appliances in the houses. Electric motors will burn up if the current is not a steady 60 cycles per second. Lights and heating elements aren't as critical, but fridges and freezers certainly are.

We had a large-faced cycle meter in the kitchen of our house so we could see exactly where the power was and make adjustments if necessary.

With any kind of electrical generation for residences, the 6 p.m. to 8 p.m. hours are the highest usage, and if we made it through that time period we were good for another 24 hours.

Ours wasn't the only small hydro plant in the area, but it was the only high-head plant operating with limited water. One other ranch had a wheel that had been installed so long ago that it used wooden pipe. This was definitely a low-head machine, as wooden pipe would never take the pressure that our steel pipe could. After we installed this system it opened up the possibility for some others in the area, and we helped with their design.

After almost ten years of continuous use, the incoming pipe started leaking a little, so we shut it off and encased the 20 feet coming into the house in cement. When we uncovered the pipe we discovered that the leaks were the result of vibration; only the welded joints were leaking. After pouring the cement we left the system off for a week to let it cure. Turning it back on too soon might have vibrated the wet cement enough to restart the leak. The system was quite noisy right from the start, noise we had attributed to the water hitting the wheel. But after the cement was put in, the machine was nearly silent. We had been hearing the vibrating inlet pipe.I don't remember the name of the very small company that made our wheel, but it was located in Custer, Washington. They custom-make their Pelton wheels to fit your situation, considering the fall and flow of your water and how much electricity you need to generate. As I look back, we didn't even give them any actual specs, only general ideas.

The intake for these systems is also very critical. It's important to filter out the trash that floats down the creek, or the nozzle will plug. When we needed to work on the system we shut off the water and let the system drain, because I sure didn't want to work with 200 psi water in the pipe!

Someone had given me an old Mother Earth Journal and I got most of the calculations from that. The system in that article was much smaller than what we wanted, but I was able to use the calculations for fall, water amounts, and rpm.

Higher up in the mountains, there was a small hay meadow that we flood-irrigated. We put the Pelton intake right at the bottom of that meadow to catch all the waste water. Next, the water went down the hill and through the system, and after the system it went into a mainline pipe to gravity-sprinkle the fields below the house. That water was used three times in less than two miles. The neighbors teased us about wearing out our irrigation water before we let it go!

## CHAPTER FOUR

# RANCHING AT EMPIRE

In Chapter 1, I wrote about the problems of operating at 7,500 feet in Colorado. I decided the solution was to sell the high mountain ranch and look for one with a longer grazing season. This led me on the trail to greener pastures and eventually B.C. The B.C. drawing card for me was the fact that along the Fraser River, in the lower elevations, cattle could be grazed out all winter due to the shallow snow and coastal chinook winds. This move allowed us to cut our hay feeding by about five months, from seven in Colorado to two in B.C. That didn't completely eliminate the price squeeze, given that we still needed all the hay machinery, but we would cut our inputs.

**An Empire hay meadow**

The problem with the winter range in B.C. was not snow, but ice. When the coastal chinook winds came in January, they melted the snow, but the next freezing night would cover every steep hill with ice. The trails going down embankments to water had lots of gravel. Getting to the barn, though, could be tricky. On some mornings, the cowboys had to crawl to the barn on all fours after taking a nasty fall on the ice. (As long as no one actually got hurt, watching the process provided a lot of amusement.) Once they got to the barn, the rest of the day would be okay because their horses were sharp-shod and had no difficulty with the ice.

Any time you change ranches, you face some changes in management. This is true whether you move next door or to another country. You have to add up the special features of your new ranch and quickly figure out what class of cattle will work best on that particular operation. When we moved to Empire we faced these decisions in spades. For example, we needed stock that could winter out and not eat up the hay we were saving for our future cow herd.

Empire hay operation

The first year we decided to rest most of the range. We hadn't purchased a cow herd, and the few cattle and horses we had moved from

Colorado could easily spend the summer on the pastures close to the headquarters. A compressed operation would also eliminate the need for a large crew, which we didn't have at that point.

We have always relied heavily on the advice of our new neighbors to help with such decisions. They have often observed what has been successful in the past or things they might have done differently. A neighbor, Jack Koster, had run yearlings on Empire and strongly recommended the same to us. In fact, he wanted me to run yearlings and a large purebred herd of Horned Herefords so we could supply bulls to ranches in a large area of B.C. that had been getting their bulls from Alberta. He assured us he would buy all his bulls from us. This proposal interested us enough that we went down to Washington to buy enough cows to build a herd. We visited several available herds and then found an older gentleman who had a very prominent herd of line-bred Mark Donalds. We opted not to go that direction, but I have since regretted that decision.

Churn Creek grassland

The first thing we tried was the purchase of light yearling steers to winter over and then fatten the next spring and summer. This worked really well, as the light yearlings were old enough and tough enough to survive the winter and then explode in the spring. Calves just weren't tough enough to make it through the winter on dry grass. Cows did fairly well, but they would lose condition from the cold and lack of water. Amazingly, they seemed to bounce right back after a day or two on decent water.

Mounted cowboys work cattle in Empire corrals

After the yearling steers we tried light, open, yearling heifers. We bred them in the spring after they wintered out and then sold them as bred coming-three-year-olds in the fall. They were fairly fleshy and commanded a good premium since they were coming threes. We were able to buy several hundred from a neighbor across the river and trail them home. They did well and bred very well, and we sold them the next fall.

I sold them to an order buyer I had dealt with in the past, and we delivered the heifers to a holding lot in Kamloops. I went home and the next week expected a check, but nothing came. I called the buyer, and he said it would be coming for sure next week. Next week, same thing; no check. I called and got the same runaround as before. This time I packed, told the family I would be back when I had the money, and headed to town. There was a lot of money involved, so I needed a resolution to the matter. I called the buyer before I got into Kamloops, and he persisted with the same old story. I found his home address and was parked in front of his house bright and early the next morning. He came out and headed to a restaurant where he met for coffee and made deals with many of his customers. After he was seated at a booth, I sat down in the next booth. He came over and asked what I wanted. I told him I wanted the money and he could expect to see me in his rear-view mirror everywhere he went until he paid me. He didn't say much and had to leave to meet with another customer.

He seemed kind of nervous. After his restaurant meeting we headed out for his day's travels. I followed him everywhere he went until late in the afternoon. Finally, he came over to me and said he would take me to where the money was. I followed him into a main hotel downtown, and he introduced me to two men that he said he worked for. He told them what I wanted, and they told him to let me have my money. He said that he didn't have it and that it was being held by an auction yard in Alberta. We called the yard right then and there, and the auction owner said that he was holding the money pending more cattle coming from me. I said that he already had them all, and he said he would send the money. In the end, I went to my bank manager and had him contact the auction owner's bank, and they worked out an immediate transfer. Relief at last.

After a few weeks I learned that the two men in the hotel had come to Kamloops to figure out what this buyer was doing with their money. He had been selling cattle for them and not paying them and claiming they had more cattle in the holding lot than were actually there. In the meantime, he was using the money to cover gambling losses.

Soon after this, we knew we had to find a cow herd for Empire. We went to several dispersions but couldn't compete, given the B.C. subsidy (which we didn't qualify for). At one of these sales a young cow buyer approached me and said he had a nice herd of cows for sale just down the road four miles. We immediately went to look at them and really liked what we saw. We bought 400 cows aged three to eight that were as even as you could ever hope for. My only regret was that I didn't buy every cow and bull on the place that day to start our herd. They were for sale because the ranch owner had sold the ranch to BC Hydro and then leased it back, and the lease was running out. These were the TJ cows, and they were absolutely the finest bunch of commercial cows I have ever owned.

Empire cattle drive

We loaded them and headed home. When we unloaded at the suspension bridge over the Fraser, one old hide dived off the road and went straight to the river, our foreman right behind her. When she got down to the river, she just trotted right across the ice to the other side. The foreman went after her and brought her back. Had I seen what he was doing, I would have stopped him, because he could have broken through the ice at any time. Besides the danger of falling through, the river ice was very thick and rough and dangerous. As the river froze upstream, ice chunks would break off and float downstream until they hit other ice. At that point, large pieces would turn up and freeze in place, standing on edge. Crossing such ice was extremely hazardous, not only because of the jagged surface but also because much of the ice was too thin to support a man's weight.

Now she was back on the right side of the river, but she wouldn't come back up to the road, so we had to take hay down to her every day. One day I was carrying some hay down to feed her when she started up the trail, intending to do us harm. I heard the foreman behind me stop, turn around and then hoof it up the hill away from the charging cow. I figured she would stop at the hay, so I just stayed where I was. Sure enough, when she got to the hay she stopped to eat, and we escaped harm. Later, when I caught up with the foreman, he said, "I wanted to stay, but my feet wanted to go!"

Another strategy we used had to do with the timing of our cow sales. We had visited several packers and asked them when they would pay a premium for old cows that had been culled in the late fall. The answer was always the same: they would definitely pay a good premium between Christmas and New Year's. They had to kill every day, but there were no auctions selling during that period, and they really needed the cows. This worked so well that we did that for years and years. Several of these packers stockpiled cows in feedlots just to have them when they needed them, so we found the ones that weren't doing the stockpiling.

Later, I had a bunch of cows in a feedlot in Kamloops waiting for the New Year's jump in the old cow market. But when I went to get them, the RCMP had everything in the lot locked and guarded. They were inventorying the entire lot to figure out discrepancies in the buyer's count.

# RANCHING AT EMPIRE

The only bad thing was that the cows were locked up for a whole month, and the feed costs kept rolling.

One of the complications at Empire was lack of grain. Today I would probably develop them on hay alone, but at the time the competition from Alberta would have been in the fat department.

Feeding cattle at Empire

I did start selling bulls from our purebred herd of 50 head, and Jack, true to his word, bought all the bulls we could sell him. Normally he took all our bulls six years and older that we had already used. This arrangement worked very well for both of us.

Another neighbor, Gene Mooney, was a descendant of the famous Chisholm Trail family. Gene wrote me one April and wanted three bulls delivered to his corrals at Big Bar. He sent a check in the mail and I was to deliver them on the 25th of May.

Gene's ranch presented some interesting transportation challenges. His place lay on the west side of the Fraser River; the road was on the east side, and there was no bridge, so the only way to get to his place was by ferry. To get to town in the summer he would ride out to the ferry, put his horse on board, and cross the river to a car he stored for that purpose, leaving his horse in a corral for the ferry operators to feed until his return.[4]

He wanted the bulls delivered to the corrals on the west side of the river. His corral was a half-day ride from his house, and he needed to drive them home. To get there I had to drive onto the ferry (not much bigger than my truck) and cross the river to the corrals on the west side. In late May, the Fraser is in flood stage; very large tree root clumps were floating down the river at seemingly high speed. With some luck (providence, really) the ferry operator managed to guide us through them safely. Then he waited for me until I came back from the corral.

Big Bar ferry with load of hay for back country

In the winter, Gene crossed the quarter-mile-wide river in a basket suspended from the same cable the ferry used in the summer. In the fall, they would pack, on horses, enough gas and kerosene to last through the winter. They had a Honda generator that powered the TV and a few lights at night.

Of course, we had our own transportation difficulties. Our first test came when we ordered that load of yearlings our first year at Empire. I had called a buyer named Slim and told him I needed about 400 light Horned Hereford yearling steers. Some time later, the phone went out for two weeks, and with the other projects going on I almost forgot about the order. Finally the phone came back online and a call came

---

[4] On one occasion Gene ordered a tractor, baler, mower, and rake, all of which had to be lowered on a cable down a cliff by a Cat.

through that the trucks would be at the bridge the next day. We went into panic mode getting ready. We had to haul horses and hay down to the river to get the steers, overnight them, and then drive them up into our winter range in Churn Creek Flats[5].

After we had overnighted the steers at the river, we trailed them five miles up the mountain to the winter pasture and scattered them out. It was late November and there was little snow on the ground, but by year's end the snow had gotten deep enough that we had to bring them home. The water had also frozen up and they were beginning to shrink. We wanted to keep the inputs low, but we didn't want to lose any calves or critters.

The first day we gathered 377, which meant we were short 23. We looked for several days and found 20 that had drifted to higher ground, where they could go from tree to tree and eat the grass under the overhang of the tree. Now we were looking for three. We had ridden the pasture for several days to no avail when Bob Muncey, from the Gang, offered to fly us around and look from the air. It was a beautiful flight, even at 15 degrees below zero. We spotted two of the largest mule deer bucks either of us had ever seen (which was quite a few between the two of us).

We also found some steers, and that made my day. Later I decided to make another swing through the rough country and have one more look. I used a tractor we had chained up for the trip so I could cover more ground and not wear a horse out. Back at the far end of the pasture I spotted a line of tracks in the snow about 200 yards away. They looked

---

[5]The steers were 18 months old. They were purchased at the sale yards in Williams Lake and had come from the Chilcotin region, west of there. That area is famous for raising light long yearlings that are all frame and no fat, perfect for wintering out, large enough to survive yet mature enough to really put on pounds when the green grass came. These steers did very well, and we sold them the next August at 1050 pounds. They had arrived at about 625, so they had a gain of a little over a pound per day, with no inputs other than interest and labor. There was a very good market in Alberta for two-year-old steers ready for finishing. In the early days operators in our area fattened steers on this grass and them sold them to packers in Vancouver. Each fall they would corral the steers, and the packer buyer would cut through them and pick the slaughter-ready animals. The rest would go back out on the range and go through the same process the next year until they made the grade.

like horse tracks, but I knew that no horse had gotten further than me that morning. When I got close I discovered large, dog-like tracks.

The tracks were huge, as large as those of a big horse. The only thing that could have made tracks that large was a lone wolf. Since then, whenever someone tells me they aren't sure if the tracks they had seen were a large coyote or a wolf, I always say if it's a wolf track you won't wonder in the least.

I looked over one very steep hill and saw several steers eating the grass that some bighorn sheep had just uncovered by pawing the snow aside. The steers would eat until the grass was gone and then butt the sheep away from the freshly uncovered grass and eat there. It was almost as if the sheep were helping the steers, because they could have left the area at any time and the steers would have starved.

Later, we rebuilt the fence along the winter pasture. The crew foreman had to drive roofing nails through the soles of the boots of the crew to keep them from sliding down the steep hillside and out of the pasture. The foreman was a laid-off worker, as this was a government make-work project. He had been a manager at the local Caterpillar store. Since he had recently been promoted he could be fired, but the other workers could not because they had a union contract.

I will never forget driving those first steers up the road to the hay fields and watching the steam rising from them to form a little cloud.

At one time I dropped some salt blocks from a plane into those steep basins to coax the steers there to utilize the good grass. You had to fasten your seat belt and be prepared for wind, with one door of the plane removed. Later I learned that it was much easier to just roll the blocks off the steep hill, having first made sure no steers or sheep were in the way.

Gang Ranch had a pasture across the river from our house that I really wanted. It could winter 800 cows out every year, all winter long. The only drawback was that you had to keep a man down there in the river to chop the ice and gravel the banks of the river so the cattle could water. This man had to live in a gold miner's dugout in the bank more than 20 miles from his nearest neighbor, so very few hardy loners could handle that job.

In our hay operation, we went from stacks to small, square bales to Hesston stacks to mid-size big bales. Almost all these transitions were market-driven. The only exception was the move to Hesston stacks, a change we had made before leaving Colorado in an effort to stop hay theft. We were plagued with thieves because we were so spread out and fairly close to towns with lots of horses. We moved the Hesston to B.C. and it fit right in, as there were already lots in use in the area. At Empire, we used small bales to feed the horses at the barn and whenever the stack feeder broke down. I tried feeding stacks by hand, but only once. The hay was so tight I had to peel off a whole layer while standing on the stack. Imagine trying to fork off army blankets while standing on top of them and you've got the picture.

Stack wagon haying system

Tom loading bales at Empire

Hook family stacking bales at Yodel cow camp

Sophie, the previous owner at Empire, had left an old baler as part of the repossession deal. I believe it was a John Deere 24T. It was truly worthless. I was taking it to town to trade one day, and as I passed Jack Koster's fields I noticed a brand new John Deere baler in the field, hooked to one of his tractors. I decided it might be fun to hook my worthless old baler up to his tractor and pull his new baler around behind the stack to hide it. I could just envision the look on Jack's face when he said, "It sure looks like this fellow has made himself quite a nice trade." It was a fun idea, but I never got around to implementing it. There was also a lot of needle and thread grass but almost no planted or improved grasses. The provincial government of B.C. had a big program pushing a no-till-in crested wheat grass. At first it looked very good, but within five years it was totally gone. That was a very big disappointment to everyone, and I never heard the scientific reason why it failed so completely. We didn't have any of this done, as most of our lower country was too steep and rough to plant mechanically.

The higher-elevation grasses were mountain brome or pine grass, but mostly native short-season summer grasses. The pine grass was almost totally unusable except when cattle were nearly starved, in heavy snow conditions. Under those circumstances they would dig through the snow and eat it. The mountain brome was great and grew mostly around the birch tree meadows. The downside to the mountain brome was that wherever it grew, there seemed to also be a lot of timber milk vetch, a plant very lethal to milking cows (although their calves were unaffected).

We were able to graze out between nine and ten months of the year. I mentioned above that Gang had a winter pasture across the river that grazed 800 cows all winter, but our side was just enough higher and more snow-covered during January and February to require some feeding. We put up about 1,500 tons of hay, mostly alfalfa, with some brome and timothy mixed in. When the Maytags operated Empire, they purchased a lot of hay, but it was always a problem trucking to that side of the river. Whenever we were short we sent the weaned calves out to Kamloops or Armstrong, to backgrounding lots. This way they

Tom, Kenneth Shenk and Tom's father, Lee Hook, survey new hay fields

were already out and available for shipping if the market cooperated.

You could grow corn there, for silage. Some of the neighbors did for a while, but they didn't keep it up very long because it was a bit dicey. The gardens would grow everything but melons. There was even an abandoned tomato processing plant near Kamloops. The growing season was pretty short, about 70 days, but the summer days were very long, so that made up somewhat for the short season. Someone had planted apricot trees, but they were all wiped out one winter by a six-week spell of -55 degrees Fahrenheit. There were a lot of grapes grown around Kamloops, and now a lot of ginseng is raised.

We were at Empire when the ultrasound imaging equipment came on the market. A salesman from somewhere in eastern Canada called the Gang Ranch and wanted to demonstrate it on their 3,500 cows. The same salesman called me to see if they could also use us for a demonstration for what they hoped would be a sale.

The man flew across the country to Williams Lake. Then he drove two hours on a nasty dirt road to get to the Gang headquarters. When he arrived, they said they would have to take him back into the mountains where the cows were, and that would take another two hours in a four-wheel-drive truck. They made the trip okay and were ready to start the pregnancy checking. The salesman got the machine out and started hooking it up when he discovered he had brought the pig probe rather than the cattle probe. He almost cried, as he had spent nearly two days getting to the cows and had another two days ahead of him to go home. Four days and not a single test!

At Empire, our cattle were vulnerable to predators, large and small. Eagles were an occasional issue; bears were a big problem. I'll have more to say about both in a later chapter. But the most problematic predators were the smallest: ticks.

The ticks were a variety only prevalent in the Northwest, I think. They caused paralysis. They could immobilize an animal and literally drop it. Just one tick could paralyze an animal if attached in the right spot: between the back of the head and the top of the shoulders, on a narrow line above the spinal cord. The tick would inject an anticoagulant into the host to draw blood. The minuscule amount of fluid included a paralyzing substance that dropped the animal in its tracks.

When we found a critter that had fallen victim to a tick, it would be lying perfectly flat with its eyes open but unable to move anything connected to the spinal cord. The ticks didn't actually kill the animal; they died when birds pecked out their eyes, or when found by bears or coyotes. Only yearling cattle seemed to be affected. Cows and calves were immune, although horses, dogs, deer, and humans were susceptible. Sometimes there would be a ball of ticks the size of your fist protruding about a half inch from the animal's hide. If you were able to find and remove the one offending tick, out of dozens, the animal would get up immediately and be as good as new.

Paralytic ticks on Empire yearling

At first we sprayed the yearlings just as we turned them out, but the first little shower washed off the spray, requiring us to gather them from the 15,000-acre pasture and spray after every shower. Then we found a pour-on product called Dursban which had a much longer useful life. One treatment always seemed to be enough.

Dursban was legal in Canada and the U.S., but Canada prohibited importing more than eight ounces, or $40 worth. This prevented dealers from importing it, so we had to buy it in the U.S. and import it ourselves. We had to respect the restrictions, but we heard about a solution someone had figured out. About a month before we needed to treat our yearlings, I would go down to the coast and check into a motel as close as possible to a border crossing. I would cross into the U.S. and purchase a case or two of Dursban. I would take those cases to an all-night service station very close to the crossing and ask if I could leave the boxes there overnight. Then I would take out one bottle, cross the border, take it to the motel, and head back across for another bottle, to repeat the routine. Since it took several trips, I usually did this at night when the border crossings weren't too busy and I could check through quickly.

One night, I had just started the importation and an elderly agent was checking me through. I noticed he was always sitting in a chair reading the paper when I drove up. He had to get up every time to check me through. After four or five interruptions to his reading, he asked, "Just how many more trips are you going to make?" I told him I would cross 31 more times during the night. He asked why I only brought one at a time, as he was getting tired of me. I explained the importation regulations, assuring him that what I was doing was perfectly legal. Hearing that, he told me to put the rest of the cases in my car, bring them across and get the heck out of his otherwise peaceful evening. I did just as he suggested. On my last trip he waved me through, I got some sleep, and the next morning headed home.

Later we used rope wick oilers. We built three-sided pens, hung the oiler across the fourth side, and then put the salt or mineral in the pen, where the yearlings would have to go under the oiler to get any salt. This finally solved the problem for us once and for all.

To reach either Empire or Gang Ranch required crossing a suspension bridge over the Fraser River. It was a major bottleneck for both ranches, for two reasons. First, the approaches involved very tight 90-degree turns. In addition, the bridge had a 27-ton weight restriction. Normal cattle liners or pots couldn't get onto the bridge from the east. What we call a truck and pup (or actually an A-train) could just manage to navigate the bridge, but it had to be less than half loaded.

Fraser River suspension bridge

This required a lot of shuttling cattle from a corral on the west side (built for that purpose) to the trucks waiting on the east side. The truck had to leave the pup on the east side, cross the bridge and drive 18 miles to the ranch. After loading, the driver would take the cattle back down, cross the bridge, and unload into the pup. Then he would come back to the ranch, load again, head back down, cross, hook up to the pup, and head out. This process took all day. Any feed came in the same way, by breaking up a B-train at the bridge and then shuttling the feed up to the ranch. Needless to say, we never got the same trucker twice!

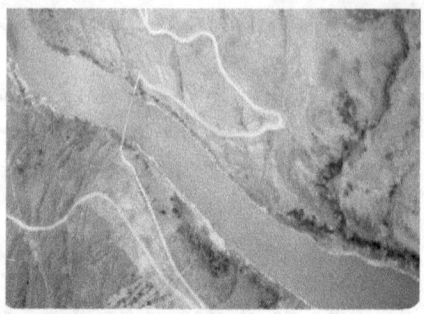

Fraser bridge aerial view

After we bought Empire we purchased a trailer to haul our cattle across this bridge. We used it to move all our furniture, appliances, and personal possessions from Colorado. It was designed to allow the installation of 4x8 plywood sheets to keep dust and water out. The plywood could be removed for normal open slats to haul cattle.

Another difficulty semi-trucks had in approaching the bridge was the overhead suspension cables anchored into the bank. To turn

Tom's semi navigating Fraser River bridge on moving day

the corner onto the bridge you had to swing wide and stay as close as possible to the steep bank on the left. But at that angle, the cables hung too low. Our straight trailer was lower than the liners, and its short wheelbase made it very maneuverable. Even then, the front of the trailer top almost scraped the cable on the turn. If the tractor exhaust pipe happened to be situated on the driver's side, it always got bent. We learned to look for this when a driver pulled into our yard. When we saw a shiny chrome exhaust pipe bent back, we knew we were in for an earful from an irate trucker.

Even with these problems, we felt blessed just to have a bridge. Two ranches down the river from us had to cross their cattle on a small ferry.

## RANCHING AT EMPIRE

They held the shippers on the west side in a set of corrals, with an alleyway about 100 feet long out to the river bank, where the ferry docked. When the ferry stopped, they lowered a ramp and the cowboys pushed 10 or 15 cattle onto the ferry, loaded their horses, and crossed the river. On the other side they drove them off the ferry into a holding pen. Then they ferried back to do it all again. Sometimes they shipped 50 or 100 cattle in this way.

In more recent times, the logging industry has built roads into these ranches from Lillooet. Now they can get their cattle to market by road. But it's a very long road. In the early days, Gang Ranch and Empire had to force their shipping cattle to swim the river to get to market. They used boats to keep the cattle headed across the river and prevent them from turning back.

Our first summer at Empire, we spent a lot of time just exploring the ranch. We needed to see everything and get a feel for how we might use the different areas. One of those areas was Magee Flats. Magee was about five miles south of the house, at a lower elevation from the headquarters but not right down on the Fraser. It was dry and hot, and had almost no stock water, so cattle seldom drifted down there. There was a road to it, but it was steep, narrow and very dangerous. In 12 years, I took only one 4x4 pickup and one small Ford tractor down there, to install oilers for the paralytic ticks. On the way out, the pickup broke a universal joint and had to sit there until we could go to town, get the part, and then put it in on the hill where it broke. When I drove the tractor there, it almost jumped off the road. To get it out of there, one man had to ride on the hood for balance. Two heads of hair were standing on end during that episode.

During that first summer I was curious about the flat, so one day I rode down on a horse. As I was wandering around the flat, suddenly a bull came from nowhere and charged the horse. I was riding a smart little cow horse who danced out of the way with no harm done. The bull immediately spun around and had at us again. This time we took off at a good speed and quickly outran the bull. After a couple hundred yards, we slowed down and looked back at the bull, but he was still coming after us as fast as he could. He couldn't travel very fast, as he was horribly bench-kneed and couldn't actually run. This time we went up the trail about a quarter-mile before we stopped, but he was still coming as fast as he could. This went on for two or three miles until he finally gave up. He was a purebred bull from a very reputable breeder and actually belonged to Sophie, the lady who had the ranch before us. I would guess the bull to be five or six years old. The same thing happened every time a rider went into that area, so we decided that the bull had to go. Since he belonged to the prior owner, I didn't feel free to just shoot him, so I called her and explained the situation. Of course she wanted nothing to do with him but said that she would like to have the meat. I said we'd see what we could do.

A few days later, a couple of the Native cowboys and I decided to go down and get the bull. We took a tractor over to the point where the road got bad and then rode the horses down to find the bull. Actually, it was more like letting the bull find us, very carefully. Before long he spotted us and came running. We knew we could outrun him easily, so we stayed just far enough ahead to be safe and yet close enough to tantalize him. Sure enough, he kept up the chase all the way to the tractor, where we shot him. We hooked a chain around his horns and dragged him back to the house, where we skinned and quartered him. We hung the quarters in the cool room. I called the lady, and in a day or so she showed up to claim her meat. I told her that we should at least give some to the cowboys, and she agreed. That carcass wasn't the prettiest, and I wanted no part of it. I knew the Natives didn't either, as we supplied them all of their meat, but they were always looking for dog food and this bloodshot meat was just what the dogs loved.

I have been around dangerous cattle all my life, and I classify them into three categories. There are the wild ones that just want to get away, the wild mean ones (like this bull) that will come and get you, and the tame ones that are mean and will get you unexpectedly. The last are what I hate the most, because they aren't afraid of you and don't give any warning.

My dad had a very good horse killed right under him by a neighbor's wild, mean bull. The sharp end of the bull's horn cut the heel of dad's boot just under the spur before goring the horse. These bulls were the worst because they were totally wild, mean, and very fast and agile.

One more story about Magee Flats. We eventually started using that area in the spring for yearlings. The Native cowboys rode down there nearly every day, looking for cattle with paralytic ticks. One year I noticed they were very faithful in riding that area nearly every day. Even members of the crew who never rode horses suddenly developed an interest in riding. Then I noticed they were all carrying binoculars. That seemed strange. After asking around I learned that the hippies from down the river liked to use a sand bar right under Magee Flats for their "all-natural sunbathing." The faithful cowboys were going there and lying on their stomachs to peer over the edge of the cliff. Of course, binoculars were at a premium around there, especially the more powerful ones. You can imagine their glee when they found out I had a 50x spotting scope that I would loan them occasionally.

## CHAPTER FIVE

# NEIGHBORS

One of the finest parts of a ranching life is the neighbors. At least, most of the neighbors.

Probably the best neighbor we ever had was a man named Jack. Jack was a big help to Connie and me when we started out with our first ranch and our first purebred cattle. Jack, and a neighbor named Stan, often helped a third neighbor with their carload of bulls at the carload show in Denver. On one of these occasions, Jack and Stan started to scuffle in the stockyards in Denver. Stan had been a boxer in the military during Korea, and Jack was as tough as they come. The scuffle against a fence grew more aggressive, and when they broke some 2x8 fence rails they decided that was enough. I never heard who won the scuffle.

Another time, Jack and his son were hauling some bulls to a rented pasture and wanted me to take a load. When I arrived at their place they were just getting ready to brand some young bulls. Jack was trying to light a kerosene branding-iron heater that stood on legs about four feet high. It was made from a ten-inch pipe with a nozzle in one end, where the flame had to be lit. Jack had his head bent around and inside the pipe so he could see to light the flame. It was just after the Fourth of July, and I had some matches and a cherry bomb in my pocket. Which gave me a bright idea. I lit the cherry bomb and dropped it at Jack's feet. When his son saw what I was doing, he took off for the far side of the barn. About that time I decided I should leave the scene of the crime, too. We heard a very loud bang, and Jack jumped straight up in the air with his head still in the heater. After the dust had settled, he had bent his glasses, torn his ear, and had a nice bump on the top of his head. Deep down I really did feel bad after I saw the damage the bomb had caused. But I never let on.

I was one up on Jack, but not for long. Sometime later I was down in the bottom of a portable feeder cleaning out mold when Jack drove by and saw his opportunity. He quietly parked, sneaked out of his truck, and picked up a 2x4, with which he hit the side of the feeder as hard as he could. Needless to say, I came up out of that feeder like a prairie dog scrambling out of his hole.

Jack and I had the greatest times working and hunting elk together.

A different Jack was a wonderful neighbor when we lived at Empire. Jack Koster was a great man I came to know and love. He has a very interesting history, being part Native and all rancher. He is a dead ringer for Sean Connery in speech, looks, and action.

In the early days, Jack's father, Henry, established the Alkali Lake Ranch in B.C. Alkali Lake is probably the finest ranch in B.C. for its size. It was there that Henry married Jack's mother, who was a resident of the local reserve.

At one time a meat company from Calgary contracted Jack's father to drive a herd of fat cattle from Calgary to Whitehorse, Yukon. The trip had to take place in the winter. The route went through Seattle, where they boarded a boat to sail up the mouth of a river as far as they could until they came to where it was frozen, where the cattle would then traverse over the ice. This route would lead them through the coastal mountains to Whitehorse. They had to store hay along the trail so they could feed every night, and place an armed guard for each pile of hay to keep the moose from eating it. When they arrived, the cattle were slaughtered. For some reason they were thinner than when they had started out in Calgary. In Whitehorse they should have ordered CAB[6] instead.

The truly amazing part of this story is that Henry Koster made this trip with one leg. He had lost the other earlier in a shotgun accident at Alkali Lake.

I also had the privilege of working closely with Jack's brother, Henry Jr. He was our realtor in B.C. and was above reproach in his dealings. Jack was simply a great neighbor and cherished friend.

---

[6] Certified Angus Beef

Men who live and work in the country around Empire tend to be stoic, and to speak no more than necessary. They could work together in the same truck all winter feeding cattle and say nothing more than "Good morning," and "See ya." That observation serves to introduce this little story about Jack. A Native man named Alec worked for Jack for many years in the '50s, and then Alec worked for me in the '80s. Alec told me this story.

Alec Rosette with Empire entrance road in background

A black bear had been killing cows, and Jack decided to destroy him. He took Alec with him. On this particular day, it was just before dark and they were separated by about a quarter of a mile, just below Meadow Lakes on Jack's range, waiting for this bear. The area had been burned-over several years before and had lots of stumps left.

Alec heard a shot ring out, obviously made by Jack. Later, when Jack came by for him, nothing was said. On the way back to the ranch, Alec's curiosity was working on him. Finally, Alec couldn't resist venturing a question about the shot, to which Jack replied with one word: "Stump." Nothing more was ever said about the incident until I brought it up to

Jack 30 years later and he gruffly said, "Keep that quiet. That little rascal was sworn to secrecy."

In January, during one particularly cold and snowy winter, Jack found a cow that had been killed by wolves. When they found her, she was lying along the edge of a very steep, high bank above the river. There was not a tooth mark on her, but the tracks in the snow told the story: the wolves had run her back and forth along the edge of that bank, trying to force her over, until she died from exhaustion.

Later in the afternoon, Jack went down to a small embankment above the cow, far enough away so as to not spook the wolves. He dug a hole in the bank where he could crawl in and wait. Just before dark, the mother wolf came back to the kill. Jack waited, hoping more would come, but finally shot her. He said he always regretted not waiting a few more minutes to see if he could have gotten two or three.

Jack was a very good hunter and had spent 80-plus years honing his skills. He died at the age of 95, in the fall of 2010.

Our very good friends and neighbors across the Fraser River to the east had a ranch called Canoe Creek. Their ground started at the Fraser River and ran about 30 miles to the east. The headquarters was located about five miles east of the river, in a small valley. At the eastern end of their range was a fenced holding pasture around some small lakes. This area was called Rocky Springs. One lake had an island where the local rancher fed cattle in the winter by driving across the ice.

One day, we were heading back to Empire along this area of small, shallow lakes when we saw a strange sight. The rancher had set out to the island but had pressed his luck too far. His pickup, loaded with hay, had broken through the ice. The truck was almost completely submerged, with just the roof of the cab and the top of the load sticking out of the water. The truck and hay stayed there for a couple of months before it got retrieved.

Trips to the vet could get interesting in that back country. Like the story in the prologue about taking the heifer into town to the vet one night. A neighbor had a similar experience. He had headed to town to get a cesarean. When he got to the clinic he backed up to the chute and went into the office. Shortly after, one of the vets came into the office and said there was no heifer in the truck. He went out and, sure enough, the tailgate was in place, but no heifer. He called home to find out if the assigned crew had indeed loaded the heifer. They were very sure that they had. So where was the heifer? He headed home and found her calmly grazing along the highway. She still hadn't had her calf. He got her into a corral, loaded her, and headed back to the vet. To this day, no one knows how that heifer got out of the truck with the tailgate still in place.

Road the road to Clinton

The road back toward Clinton was actually very good to travel, except for the dust in the summer and sometimes ice after a silver thaw. It was best when the snow was packed, with the temps below zero Fahrenheit. In times like that, there was no dust and it wasn't slick, just long.

Too long for some folks ... like the couple who came to be interviewed for a job one day. On the way back out to the highway, their car went off the road. As it happened, my wife had been to town and was coming home on the same road when she came up on their car in the ditch. When Connie walked over to see if there was anything she could do, the woman went into a tirade about how they had been to the western edge of the Earth and looked over. Nobody in their right mind could ever live out there! Connie didn't tell the lady how eager she was to get home to Empire and how much she loved living there. As someone has said, you had to love it to like it.

Another Rocky Springs story happened in the small line cabin there. The cabin was very small, but it did include a combination heater/cookstove, a table, and two folding metal cots. The cots were placed parallel, along the walls behind the stove. The place was built mostly for one-night stayovers, or just to warm up on the long ride home. Two Native riders stayed at the cabin for a while, and the rats nearly drove them nuts during the night. One rider was very affected by their presence. All the nighttime rodent activity was keeping him awake.

One particular night, this fretful Native just couldn't get any relief, so he decided to take some action. The other rider was deeply asleep in the facing parallel cot. The worrier had taken his .30-06 and a flashlight to bed. When he finally came to his wits' end, he switched on the flashlight, and sure enough there were rats under his companion's cot, four or five feet away. Without waking the sleeper, he took careful aim and fired at a rat at almost point-blank range. Of course, this put the rifle muzzle only a few feet from the near ear of the sleeping beauty. One instant, that man was sound asleep, lying prone on his cot in perfect peace, and the next instant he was standing erect on the foot of his cot, still in his sleeping bag. His eyes were wide open but not seeing anything, nor were his ears hearing. It took him some time to figure out just what had happened, especially when he couldn't hear the shooter as he tried to explain and apologize. In fact, for several months it was very hard to get his attention, and he rarely understood what he was being told. When the ringing stopped he was still deaf, but he seemed to be quite happy in a world of his own. He was married; maybe that had something to do with his bliss.

## CHAPTER SIX

# THE COWBOYS

Probably the most interesting part of life on a ranch is the people. Some of them can be real characters. At Empire we seemed to have way more than our share of these. Maybe it was because we lived in such a small community and were involved in each other's lives at a level not possible in any other kind of employment. Or maybe the isolation attracted a certain kind of person. Of course, we ourselves were perfectly normal.

It took a special kind of person to live in such isolation and remoteness. Some could handle that lifestyle and some could not. The Native people were local, so they were accustomed to the remoteness. But that didn't mean that there weren't characters among them. That's one reason I have devoted an entire chapter to our First Nations employees. (The other reason is that the vast majority of our employees were Native folks.)

A time-tested bit of advice in the southern Chilcotin[7] was to hire every person that wanted work. That way, if one day there were lots of willing workers, you could get a lot done. The next day there might not be anybody, and nothing would get done you couldn't do yourself, such as moving 20 wheel lines alone or feeding 2,000 head at 40 below, when nothing starts. Since we hired everyone who came looking for a job—you had to really want a job to come that far to apply—we went through a fairly large number of people. Some stayed 12 years; others didn't last 12 hours. Most of the short-timers were potential riders. It was interesting to watch the kinds of things that got to them, sometimes very quickly. On one occasion, less than 24 hours.

---

[7] "Empire Valley Ranch is located in what is known as the Chilcotin, defined by Wikipedia as "A plateau and mountain region in British Columbia on the inland lea of the Coast Mountains on the west side of the Fraser River."

One young man showed up to work as a horse breaker, something we were always in need of. We tried to have at least 30 horses ready to go by early March, the beginning of the riding season. If we didn't start with this many, we would be nearly out of horses by late summer. There were always lots of problems with the horses in that rough country, where they put on so many miles every day. Cinch sores, saddle blanket scalds, rock bruises, and back bites were the worst. Each cowboy had a favorite string of at least four horses for his exclusive use, as long as he was working on the ranch. We usually had lots of young, unbroken horses or could get our hands on some quickly if needed.

This man came to the back door late one evening and asked for a job breaking horses. He said he and his girlfriend had been living in an old Pontiac for over a year and he really needed work. We gave him some food and pointed him to an empty house where he and company could move in. I told him to be at the barn in the morning and we would show him what was expected. First thing the next morning, the cowboys brought in the unbroken horses, eager to see what would happen. The young man started with the first horse, one not even halter-broken, and quite an audience collected to watch. He was starting out real good, and it was apparent that he had been around unbroken horses.

After a couple of hours the audience dissipated, but I stayed for a while to watch. About this time his girlfriend made her first appearance, dressed in spike heels, a leather miniskirt, and what my wife called a halter top. It was spring, and she had quite a time negotiating the corral in those shoes. She came over to me and asked for a cigarette. I was not a smoker, so I told her to ask around. She told me that she had to have one right now and wanted to know where she could buy some. I explained that there was a small store on the reserve about an hour north, and I would draw her a map. I also told her that we could order some with next week's groceries, but that would be the soonest. She went into a small nicotine fit and mumbled something as she walked off. I told her some of the cowboys might have some "rollins" if that would help. By then it was about noon, and we broke for lunch. Right at one o'clock the young man came to the door and said that they just had to get closer to cigarettes, even if it meant living in the car, and they left. I shook my head over that experience for several days.

That was the shortest stay, but there were others who came and went with nearly the same haste, often with no explanation. We saw this pattern over a long period of time before I finally figured out what was happening. When I would send a new man to the barn to get acquainted and get some horses assigned to him, the Native riders would tell the new man all about how dangerous it was working there. He would probably be chased by a grizzly bear nearly every day. They told stories of having a Bigfoot jump up on the horse behind them. The new man would hurry, wide-eyed, back to his house, pack, and leave. Most never gave a reason for the sudden decision. The mystery was finally solved for me one day when a veteran cowboy received the usual treatment but fired right back at the Natives that he had wrestled grizzlies and had a girlfriend who looked like Bigfoot. Then I realized that the men who had left without saying anything to me probably didn't want to seem chicken.

Here are some stories about the ones who stayed.

Duane came to work for us in his early twenties. He had been raised out in the Chilcotin, so he was very familiar with the lifestyle and people he might encounter. He was pretty good at staying alone in one of the camps with the cattle and didn't need supervision. He was truly a pleasure to have around. He did not have a good dog, so he got the job on his own merits. However, there are a couple of stories about him that we all remember. One of these happened at Yodel.

Yodel was our main cow camp, the first one you came to going into the back country. It was centrally located on our summer range, 26 miles from the headquarters and much further than that from any other homo sapiens, including logging and mining camps. That translates to two hours over a very dicey road passable only from June 1 to October 15 ... and even then not for the first couple of days

Tom's dad (L) and Connie's parents at Yodel cow camp

after a rain. It was fairly steep in places and forded three or four small creeks. In addition, a large mud slide was continually creeping over the road. Nearly every year, we had to run a Cat back there and push a trail through the outer tip of the mudslide to get through with a truck. We always had to haul a full load of hay and propane to keep the camp stocked.

All the other out-camps were a half-day ride from Yodel. We spent a lot of time there in the fall, and the stays were the highlight of the year for us. We kept this camp well stocked and didn't worry about theft, since the only road to it ran through headquarters. We normally hauled supplies to the other camps on a regular basis, but in an emergency the cowboys could ride there for more supplies. We kept quite a few horses there, so that anyone in a satellite camp needing a replacement horse would only have to go to Yodel for it. There was a fairly large, fenced pasture all around the cabin to hold 10 to 15 horses from July through October.

Duane was staying alone at Yodel one summer when he made an unwelcome discovery. Someone had left the gate open, probably a fisherman on a bike. The horses were gone. He looked all around the pasture in vain. Not wanting to face that 26-mile walk in his cowboy boots, he waited around a day or two.

Finally, in utter dismay and frustration, he started the long walk, leaving very early in the morning to beat some of the heat. In the middle of the day he rested in some shade along a creek and then headed out again when it had cooled off. The whole time he was expecting to come up on the lost horses, since they would surely have headed for home along this route. He was sure he would find them in the Higgenbotham meadow just outside the outer ranch pasture fence. But they weren't there, either, so he walked the last six miles to the headquarters, arriving shortly after dark. He was limping and very sore-footed; he had developed several blisters on his feet from the ordeal.

He stayed in his house at the ranch a few days healing up, but drove up every day to the outer fence, where the horses would be held up if they had tried to come home. Much to his disappointment they never showed up. Finally, I suggested we use the plane to see if we could find them.

There were two major routes home for them, so we had a pretty big area to fly. We flew for about an hour with no luck. At that point we were beyond Yodel, so that we had to fly over the cabin to head back to the airstrip. When we were right over the cabin we saw all the wayward horses standing right in front of the cabin with their heads on the porch overhang, in the shade. I thought Duane was going to cry. I wasn't sure whether it was from the joy of finding the horses, or from the realization that his 26-mile walk had been unnecessary.

In the late fall, Duane helped feed the weaned calves and so was around the corral all the time. He was sharing a house with another young man who had a house cat. Duane liked playing with that cat and did so every evening. One day he noticed a long worm hanging out of the cat's rear end. A few days later, when we were having coffee with the whole crew in the cookhouse, Duane said he sure hoped he hadn't gotten worms from that cat. Duane was very clean in everything he did, so these sorts of things worked on his mind. For quite a while after that, every time one of the others in the crew would spot a worm in the manure, they would immediately call Duane over and ask him if that was the kind of worm he thought he had. Duane became obsessed with the idea and increasingly worried about his imagined condition. Our foreman came up with the bright idea that he had read about a natural cure for worms. He told Duane that he should eat three fresh cloves of garlic per day for three days and then take a lot of laxative on the fourth day. Duane's food order that week included the garlic and laxative, and everyone was anticipating the humor of the outcome.

After the garlic arrived, Duane kind of hung to himself at coffee. On the fourth day he didn't show up for work at all. In fact it was a couple of days before he was his old self again. He ended up taking it very well but never mentioned worms again. He did, however, throw the cat out and refused to let it back in the house.

In a large succession of people cycling through the ranch jobs, some are great and others not so much. Gordon definitely fit into the first group. When I picked Gordon up at the bus, all he had with him was a small suitcase and a saddle over his shoulder. He had come for a riding job and we were happy to get him.

It turned out that Gordon actually had many talents and quickly became an appreciated and valued member of the community. Besides cowboying he had worked as a welder on the steel structures of high-rise buildings in Vancouver, hanging out on beams 15 or more stories in the air. Thus he was an excellent welder and totally fearless.

He had also been trained as a crawler-tractor mechanic in one of the large dealerships, and his skills were very good in that area as well.

After some time at Empire, Gordon acquired a fine little heeler dog and Duane's discarded cat. The dog caused him major frustration and concern at times. He always let her sleep in his house and laid his leather chaps by the door for her to lie on. Whenever she came into heat, as she did several times, Gordon had an escort of 10 or more very friendly male dogs wherever he went. Gordon and the owners of those obnoxious males had several heated exchanges, and a bout or two of fisticuffs. The problem was never completely solved to the satisfaction of everyone involved.

When Gordon first came, he told us he had overdosed a time or two and, as a result, sometimes he would do unusual things. He was very conscious of having the right clothes for whatever job he was performing. He came to work each morning wearing what he called his "appropriate uniform" for the job of the day. This in itself was not unusual, but when he didn't know what the day's job would be, he showed up in his Sherlock Holmes outfit to investigate what needed to be done that day. As Sherlock he was complete with a curved-stemmed pipe, double-billed tweed cap, tweed jacket, vest, and gold watch chain. When the rest of us could straighten up from laughing and identify his task for the day, he would merrily whistle his way back home and change into the appropriate uniform.

The story reminds me of a couple of other accounts. Our neighbors had an employee years ago that insisted on sewing a one-inch-wide yellow stripe down the outside seams of every new pair of pants. He never went anywhere without his yellow stripes. When he was on the ranch he also carried an army bugle wherever he went. Early each morning he would blow reveille, and just before dark, taps. This went on for many years.

Another strange outfit struck my eyes one morning when I came around the corner of the storehouse on the way to the shop. A stranger was standing by the shop door wearing pink Wranglers, a silk Korean dragon jacket, and a black felt stovepipe hat. He wanted a short-term job and I hired him on the spot. He was Native and called himself Wahoo. He didn't stay long, which was too bad, as he was absolutely the best horseman I have ever been around, better even than the horsemen I have met who travel around teaching clinics. He had trained horses and mules for the Canadian military at some time in the past. Reportedly he was also one of the few men who had ever swum across the Fraser River. I understand he was inspired to this feat by the RCMP behind him. A few years later he met his untimely end when a car ran over him at a rodeo. Apparently his fluid intake contributed to his vulnerability to such a hazard.

One day I spotted quite a crowd (at Empire, that's about three people) standing around a culvert under the road to the lower ranch houses. They were taking turns looking into the culvert, so I was curious enough to go down and see what was so fascinating. When I first arrived I couldn't see anything unusual, but the onlookers told me Gordon was in the culvert. The culvert was half full with water, flowing at about 500 gallons a minute (I knew that because this ditch ran right below our hydropower house). Gordon had noticed that the culvert was partially collapsed near the middle, so, undeterred by the rush of water, he had taken a jack in there to push it back up. No one could believe he was trying that, but as I said, he was totally fearless.

Another very endearing quality of Gordon was that he just loved to "tune" on the local hippie. This one quality made him invaluable to everyone in the area.

One of our employees who became a long-time friend was Dave Lush. He came by his nickname, Big Davey, very naturally as he was 6 feet 4 inches tall (though very slender). Dave had

Dave Lush, Oregon ranch

many great talents, but he came to Empire for a riding job. He had cowboyed at Douglas Lake Ranch, guided hunters in the coastal mountains, cooked for hunting camps, and welded, but mostly driven logging and dump trucks. He was an excellent driver and logged way over a million accident-free miles. He went on to be a truck-driving and safety consultant in the B.C. trucking industry.

The other cowboys loved having Davey along for the trek into the mountains because of his great cooking. Instead of Spam, beans, venison and rice, they could look forward to a real treat every evening. Having cooked for some guided hunting camps, Davey could really come up with some great dishes from the most limited ingredients.

Dave Lush and Theron cowboying at Oregon ranch

After several years of working for us at Empire, Dave went back to trucking. But he kept in touch with us. On one occasion when we were living in Idaho, Davey stopped by. He was on one of his cross-country hauls and decided to leave his traveling companion, Pilot, with us until he made the round trip. Pilot was a border collie that traveled many miles in the passenger seat of Davey's trucks. Davey was going out to Florida, up to New York, and then back through Idaho to his home base in B.C.

While we were dog-sitting Pilot, we only let him out of the kennel for a short time each day for fear that he would take off. One afternoon, my wife let him out for his run and had to step into the house to get something. She had been inside a few minutes when the phone rang. It was Davey calling from somewhere on the East Coast to say that Pilot had run off. You can imagine Connie's perplexity. She had just seen him moments before. She asked Davey if he knew where Pilot was, and he gave her the address and name of the people who had found him. It was our next-door neighbor. Pilot was wearing a collar with Davey's number. He had run to the neighbors, who managed to capture him and called the number. We went right over and retrieved Pilot and put him back in his kennel. The whole episode lasted less than 15 minutes. Davey was hundreds of miles away but knew before we did that Pilot had gone for a walk-about, and where to.

Davey stopped by another time and didn't have Pilot along. When we asked about the dog, Davey told us the sad story. He had gone into a truck stop in Florida to take a shower. While he was showering, Pilot tore out half of the lining of the sleeper in his new Kenworth. Davey said he and Pilot had gotten a divorce at that time.

Dave Lush (standing), Pincone and Hook family cattle drive cookout

## THE COWBOYS

Another unforgettable character from our Empire days was Pinecone. Of course, that wasn't his real name. He had been called that for so many years I'm sure lots of people only knew him by that name. The Natives had probably blessed him with the name early in his cowboy career. Pinecone walked with a fairly obvious limp, rumored to have been caused by a self-sustained injury while learning the art of quick draw. While I can't prove this, it actually seemed reasonable after knowing Pinecone for some time.

Pinecone showed up in July one year and said he had to have a job. When he pulled into the ranch yard, his old pickup ran out of gas and broke down at the same time. I had been warned against hiring him because of his tendency to lose control in stressful situations, a problem that was further complicated in that you never knew what would cause him stress. Out of compassion and pity I hired him against all the advice. He did have a fine border collie that made up for many of Pinecone's shortcomings.

At that time of year we were very short of available horses; everything had already been assigned to other strings. But we finally found him a couple of mounts on Clyde Mountain who were very good at hiding out. They had been successful at staying out of sight, and thus escaping work, that far into the year (the goal of every horse, really). Pinecone threw his worldly possessions into a room in the cookhouse and headed to cow camp, where he spent the rest of the summer and fall.

When winter came, nearly all the cowboys left for warmer entertainment. But Pinecone begged to be allowed to stay in his house and pay his rent and heat by cutting firewood for the rest of the houses. This arrangement worked very well, despite his felling a small tree on the wood truck one day. The damage was fairly minor, so everything worked out.

The next spring he started riding as soon as the ground thawed. At branding he insisted that he do most of the roping, because of the pain in his shot foot. He was roping off a dandy little gelding called Ankles that could do almost anything but really lost it whenever he felt a rope

Alec and Pinecone mounted

up under his tail. Pinecone was inclined to a little showing off, either for any ladies in the vicinity or just for the others standing around. While he was making a rather flourishing catch and drag, the rope jerked up tight under Ankle's tail and he went straight up. He could buck pretty good, so Pinecone was soon airborne. He left the saddle sitting straight up and landed in almost the same position, except that one leg was curled back so that he landed on his right spur. That had to be painful. He just sat there for a moment or two as I walked over to see if he had been hurt. When I got to him he was spitting out what was left of his hand-rolled cigarette. He had bitten the cigarette in half when he hit the ground. That is the only time in my life I ever saw a man without a tooth in his head bite a cigarette in two. It was bitten off as squarely as if he had teeth, so the impact must have been pretty hard. He wasn't hurt and returned to his roping, although his limp became noticeably worse. I was concerned about this until the other cowboys told me not to worry; they had caught him walking with no limp when he thought no one was watching.

Pinecone was very fond of his siestas. One day he found a nice shady spot in some brush for a nap. Two Native riders spotted his horse and eased over to see what he was up to. They kept very quiet and soon spotted him on the ground, snoring away. They decided to have some fun. One dismounted and the other circled wide with both horses until he was out of sight of the sleeping beauty. Then the man on foot ran as fast as he could toward Pinecone and stepped right on his stomach before immediately disappearing into the bushes. As you can imagine, there was quite an expulsion of air. The runner sneaked to the waiting horses and they both rode away very carefully so as not to be heard or seen. Of course they were eager to hear Pinecone's side of the story when he returned to the ranch, but he didn't said a word. Whether he thought a moose or Bigfoot or some other creature had stepped on his stomach, they never found out.

One spring, four riders were commuting by truck to the calving barn, leaving their horses at the barn each night rather than haul them home. Four saddled horses were about one too many to squeeze into the one-ton truck. The problem was, four cowboys were about one too many to squeeze into the cab. Two were well over six feet tall, and

Pinecone weighed about 190. The fourth was a very small Native man. It was pretty crowded in there, and Burt and Pinecone carried on a running battle for several months. Sometimes they had spur fights, like a couple of fighting roosters. Watching two guys in their mid-fifties try to spur one another was a real show. One evening they began to slug it out in the cab. Lots of missed punches were landing on the smaller Native man wedged between them. Noticing this, the driver stopped and ordered the two roosters out onto the road to settle their differences. Of course the minute they got out the fight stopped, so they all piled back in and headed home. But they soon were at it again, so again the driver stopped and ordered them out. Again they refused to fight once outside the truck. Luckily for the Native man it was only three miles home, so he survived. No one even considered riding in the back; the pecking order and perceived status were too important for that.

Pinecone had a worn-out Oldsmobile station wagon that he often drove up to the calving barn, where he would leave it when he rode for the day. One evening the car wouldn't start, so he had to walk home. He talked the best Native mechanic, Eddie, into going back with him to start the car. Eddie agreed and off they went. Later, Eddie told me that when they got to the car he started to work on what he perceived was the problem, but before he could fix it Pinecone told him that the problem wasn't in that area and shoved him out of the way. Eddie went over and sat down on the grass and watched Pinecone mechanic for more than an hour to no avail. Eddie had not touched the car after he got shoved aside but patiently watched to see what might happen. They gave up and came home. The next evening the same scenario happened, with Eddie patiently watching. For four nights this ritual continued until, in utter frustration, Pinecone told Eddie to fix the car. Eddie walked over to the car and reconnected one wire and it fired right up.

I've thought about that occasion many times and still don't know which was more remarkable: Eddie's patience or Pinecone's stubbornness!

When Pinecone was working at Gang Ranch, a female rider was employed there as well. He immediately fell in love, an arrangement that worked for her, since in his infatuation he was happy to shoe her horses. The Natives teased him mercilessly. One evening, two of them went to the shop and procured a lock washer about the size that would fit the girl's finger. They took it to Pinecone's apartment, and when he answered the door they gave him the "ring" and launched into the teasing with great zest. They didn't see the girl until Pinecone finally opened the door all the way and pointed to her. This time, the joke was on them. They couldn't face the girl for weeks.

Pinecone was the source of more stories than maybe any other employee. One time he was practicing aerobatics at the spring branding. He had a very fine saddle and was mighty proud of it. He had had bucking rolls[8] added to it during the previous winter. On the way to the branding that morning he had bragged to the rest of the riders, "There's not a horse alive that could buck me off since I got these rolls." Of course, Ankles was anxious to prove him wrong, and as Pinecone again managed to get a rope under the horse's tail, that's exactly what happened, in short order. The bucking episode ended with no harm done (except for the injured pride of the rider). Anyway, after the rest of the crew had headed home and the cowboys were pairing up the branded calves and their mothers, Pinecone couldn't let it slide and again asserted his steadfast permanence in the saddle. To show he meant business, this time he purposely jerked his rope up under Ankles' tail. Of course Ankles rose to the occasion, and Pinecone was rocketed into low orbit on the first jump. This time, when he landed the fun seemed to have evaporated, and a strange quiet set in.

Sometime later, Pinecone was pushing some cows up the trail from Koster Lake toward Fareless Camp and somehow again became airborne. This time, however, instead of landing in a sitting position he landed perfectly straight, except upside-down. The trail at that point must have been rocky, as he got a nasty cut on his scalp and a bit of a concussion. One of the other riders brought him in to headquarters. The ladies cleaned his wound and decided he should be taken into Williams Lake to see a real doctor … or at least the vet.

---

[8] Padded pouches added to the front of the saddle seat to supplement the swells and help a rider stay in the saddle.

In his delirium, he insisted that he be taken in his old station wagon; if he had to stay a few days he would need transportation to the doughnut shop and a way to get home. This meant my wife had to drive the car (without air conditioning in 95-degree heat) loaded with the patient and of course his dog, Ruff (an imported canine who insisted all the windows be kept down in spite of the dust), and Nancy, our foreman's wife, who drove our truck so the ladies had a way home. Shortly after they started, Pinecone told my wife to watch Ruff carefully. He was very prone to car sickness and if he started to drool, she must stop immediately and let him out.

It was a long, hot, dusty trip, with five or six stops for Ruff to regain composure. But they made the delivery and all went well.

Pinecone's story has a happy ending. He eventually married a very nice lady and took up the profession of maintenance man at some logging camps where his wife worked as cook.

No discussion about the crew at Empire would be complete without mentioning Burt, a character who came to Empire from Gang Ranch. Burt came to break horses, and he was very knowledgeable in this area, as well as fearless around any kind of horse.

Burt had two faults. Although he was tall and very thin, he ate more than anyone I have ever seen. I went to town with

**Pinecone and Ruff**

Burt one time and we arrived at a restaurant for breakfast. Burt ordered two of the largest breakfasts on the menu. They set two in front of him and he slicked them up in a second and probably wanted more. We learned to increase the groceries to any mountain camp where he would be staying.

We could live with Burt's eating. The real problem was his incessant talking, especially of the bragging variety. The rest of the crew tried their best to avoid him, but that wasn't easy. He lived in the house situated highest in the yard and could see everything going on. The screen on his front door was missing and he would stand against it, leaning out to get a panoramic view. From this vantage, he was ready to pounce on any potential victim on a second's notice. He always began with an ear-piercing whistle to alert his "prey." Then he would hurry down to the victim, who sadly and quietly awaited his fate. Burt would launch into his lengthy oratory on whatever subject he had prepared for the occasion. The rest of the crew would then come out of hiding and chuckle as they passed the captor and his victim.

When Burt first arrived he said he wanted me to find several four-year-old horses that had never been halter-broken and let him start from scratch. I found what he wanted across the river and we went after them, drove them into the stock truck, and hauled them home. There were three or four head in the bunch, and the next morning he announced that he was going to break them all that day. He started by roping, bridling, and saddling the first one. As soon as the saddle was tight he literally leaped on and hollered to open the corral gate. He wanted to let her run. The horse sort of half-ran and half-bucked right through a cluster of old farm machinery without mishap. Finally, she broke into a run, and Burt just let her go until she winded and stopped. Then he headed her around and brought her back to the corral. He did all the others like that the same day.

Later in the afternoon he was astride the third or fourth horse and it ran over to where I was cleaning a ditch with a Caterpillar. The horse ran out of wind near the Cat, so we visited for a bit. When the horse had rested she jumped into the ditch and tried to climb the bank on the uphill side. The bank was steep, so she fell back into the ditch and tumbled around for a while. When she had started to scramble up the bank, Burt calmly stepped off and stood there beside her while she thrashed about in the ditch. When he saw that she was about to get up he just stepped into the saddle, and off they went for another run.

Burt rough-broke all of them that first day, and I must say they have been some of the best horses we have ever had. One is still alive and lives a plush life of retirement right out in front of our present house. A few days ago, we were trying to figure out how old she is and came up with a birth year of about 1982, so that makes her 28. For many years she was our distance horse at Empire. I would hate to have to figure out how many miles she has traveled.

We weren't the only people who considered Burt something of a character. Several years later, one of the other members of the crew wanted to track him down, so he called some of Burt's ex-wives. After getting a very irate cussing out from each, he decided there must be a better way to locate the unpopular former husband.

Burt had suffered some major accidents in his life, though not one was related to his fearless approach to horses. He died some time ago at a fairly young age, from cancer I believe.

When you live in the "outback," as you might say we did at Empire, you never know just what or who you're going to run into. We had been warned to never take a photograph of anyone without their permission, as it might be dangerous. Many people try to hide (from the law, for example) by disappearing from civilization, believing they will never be found. Actually, the wilderness is the worst place to hide. So few people lived out there that anyone new stuck out like a third ear on a new calf. Any newcomer immediately triggered the moccasin network, and within a very short time everyone knew all about him.

We always needed employees, but especially experienced men that could live in the back country and somewhat off the land. They were often one or two days' horseback ride from the nearest vehicle, in a place where they needed to stay at least a month.

Several of the local men who weren't the best cowboys were hired for their dogs. The dogs became as well known as the men; often the dog was the best part of the team.

For several years we had a standing order with Employment Canada for experienced cowboys. We interviewed some interesting individuals they referred to us but never actually hired any of them.

One was a fairly young Frenchman with a small family (including a wife who spoke no English), who showed up one day in May to interview for a job. While the man and I went into the cookhouse for the interview, his wife went into our house to visit my wife. I still don't know what they talked about for two hours, given that neither knew one word of the other's language!

This tall, lanky applicant looked like maybe he could take care of himself in our setting, so we had a fairly long visit about his experiences. He was very intense and somewhat nervous. It was also obvious that he liked the sound of his own voice. I was feeling fairly positive about him as we went along, until he said, "I maust tell you dat I shoot da man!" I thought it might be a good idea for him to elaborate on that, so he did. He said he had been down in the States and gotten involved with a local girl. She had another admirer, who challenged him to a shootout. It sounded like a scene from the Old West. The Frenchman told me, "He shoot me in da foot, and I shoot heem in da head." He headed back to Canada in some haste and planned to never again venture south of the border. He said he was wanted in the U.S. but not in Canada, since he hadn't been identified.

After this exchange I told him I would contact him if he had gotten the job. But I decided against hiring him because of his nervousness, intensity, and excitability. It proved to be a good decision. In November of the same year I heard he had gotten a job with a guide out in the Chilcotin, west of us. While there, he got into an argument with his employer and shot him. Since then I have always been thankful he told me about shooting "da man," glad I decided against hiring him, and relieved to have one less hole in my hide.

Two other men who worked at Empire admitted to me, after they had been on for some time, that they had killed someone. At least one was still wanted in the U.S. He had been on a reservation in Arizona and got involved in some kind of Spiritism ritual and killed another participant. I believe this man eventually went to federal prison over an incident with the RCMP. He may still be behind bars. I don't know the end of his story, or what happened to the Frenchman, but I did hear that the third killer died of natural causes.

Near the confluence of Churn Creek and the Fraser River sat a small, dilapidated cabin that was a magnet for individuals fleeing from the law. A young man took up residence there for a while, and during that time I got a call from the RCMP. Had I seen him there, and if so, would I keep an eye on him for them? When I asked them what I would be watching for, they said he was wanted as a witness, or even an accessory, to a murder over in Alberta. They felt as long as he stayed put, that was the best place for him until the trial. I said, "Okay, but remember you owe me one."

Before satellite TV, the biggest entertainment in the remote country was trying to drive some poor crazy fool even crazier.

Confluence of Churn Creek and the Fraser River

One neighbor had a hired hand who tended to forget things. Like removing the gasoline hose before he drove away from the storage tank. He jerked the valve out of the tank, and 2,000 gallons of gas ran down the road.

Speaking of gasoline, we had a man who bragged on and on about the fuel economy of his new Honda Civic. It got so tiresome we had to do something. We came up with the idea of adding a gallon or two to his tank when he wasn't around. Of course his mileage jumped, as well as his bragging, but at least now we were all chuckling. After several months of this we decided to syphon gas out instead of adding it. Needless to say, the bragging abruptly stopped and he never said anything again. The problem was solved, so we stopped the syphoning. Actually, I think some of the Natives continued the practice for some time. I would hear them complain about the gas-line antifreeze he was using. It was eating the skin on the inside of their mouths.

In Chapter 2, I introduced our foreman, Steve Oswald. Before we moved to B.C., Steve came to work for us in Colorado.

Steve (Empire foreman) & Nancy (schoolteacher at Gang Ranch) Oswald

He started as a fence builder and, being a perfectionist, was very good at it. He had had some tough setbacks in life and kind of dropped out of society for a while. At the time he was single and, I believe, living in a teepee on a mountaintop in southern Colorado. When we moved to Empire, we asked Steve if he would manage the Colorado operation, and he agreed.

He did a great job and later expressed a desire to join us in Canada if possible. It took two years to secure his immigration status. In the meantime, he had met and married a young lady by the name of Nancy. They moved together to Empire and started their Canadian experience.

Steve was basically the foreman for the whole operation but mainly worked with the crops, fences, and with the cattle in the winter. He fit in very well with the local Natives and was possessed with enough of a sense of humor to lead them without crying.

We had hired a young man to do some riding and fence building, so Steve went out to inspect his fencing project one day. The fellow had just put in the posts for a brace for the fence. Steve was visiting with him and, while he talked, leaned against one of the posts. It had been put in so shallow that the post fell over, taking Steve with it. It's not hard to imagine the discussion that followed, especially given what a perfectionist fence builder Steve was.

During his time at Empire, Steve took up the business—maybe hobby is the better word—of beekeeping. He was continually finding another hive of wild bees in old buildings and hollow stumps and trying to capture them. This beekeeping endeavor quickly made him an enemy of the bears, although I don't remember his having any losses along that line.

Nancy became the teacher at the Gang Ranch school and was very successful in that position. She bravely drove 18 tough miles each way every day for several years. She did very well but had a few close calls. Nancy has since started writing books and is very good at that, also.

Eventually Steve and Nancy returned to Colorado to run her father's ranch, where they have made a very interesting operation.

# CHAPTER SEVEN

# FIRST NATIONS

As I mentioned earlier, nearly all our employees at Empire were First Nations members from the Shuswap (Secwepemc) people. No history of Empire Valley Ranch would be complete without sharing some of their stories.

A great deal of misunderstanding and misinformation about indigenous people floats around in other cultures. To us, they are the dearest friends and most loyal companions you would ever hope to have. They laugh more than the rest of us, and their sense of humor is truly remarkable, given the conditions under which most of them live. They seem to be entirely free from the pride that besets the rest of us, in that they can laugh at themselves and enjoy the antics of their daily lives.

Some of the stories are humorous and some bring a tear, but they are all told with the greatest respect for these fine people. Our employees at Empire lived in ranch housing, an arrangement that allowed us to see how they lived and what their humor was like. Empire is situated literally between two Shuswap reserves, Dog Creek and Canoe Creek. I can picture the naming of Canoe Creek but have always been puzzled about how Dog Creek got its name.

Sometimes a story is funny because of some disaster that almost, but didn't quite, happen. One time we were invited by one of our dearest friends, Eileen, to go to Dog Creek, about 45 minutes away over a very treacherous mountain road. The occasion was her graduation ceremony for completing high school. She was about 25 at the time. We went to the graduation, followed by dinner and a dance in the reserve gymnasium. The dancing, and the drinking, were progressing, but all in all it was a fine time.

Later in the evening one middle-aged, rather attractive Native woman seemed to acquire a fancy for me. I thought it might be best not to stick around, so we prepared to leave. But two rather large Natives blocked our way at the door and said, "No good go now!" It seemed most prudent to comply, so we did. But there was still the problem of the amorous woman. Finally, Eileen came over to explain why we were not allowed to leave. It seems Johnny C. had had a little too much to drink, had climbed the hill outside with his .30-30, and was shooting at anyone who came through the door. There was the alternative of the back door, but our truck was parked in front and we weren't eager to dive for it right under the gunman's nose. For a while I was caught between unwelcome advances and uninvited gunfire. After quite some time the "all clear" was given: the gunman had fallen asleep. No one was shot, but I heard the gunman nearly froze to death in his sleep. With the commotion the woman became distracted, and all ended well.

 I saw Johnny from time to time after that memorable occasion. In fact, he helped us trail cattle back into the mountains once. Every time I saw him, I was sure he was going to bleed to death through his eyeballs. Whether there was any correlation between his bloodshot eyes and his night of infamy on the hill with a .30-30, I never figured out.

 Jiggs was a Native cowboy who was born at Gang Ranch, lived there all his life, and rode for them many, many years. Jiggs was pretty short and lightweight, but his most noticeable characteristic was his skin color. Although Native, he was extremely fair-skinned. I would venture to say that he looked almost like an albino. Every part of him was much whiter in color than a Caucasian. His face was a very slight pink from spending years in the saddle. Jiggs also had only one eye. He wore a glass eye for many years, although he had stopped using that by the time I met him. But his years of wearing the glass eye produced another great cowboy story.

 During that time, Gang Ranch hired a young non-Native cowboy who was pretty green and totally new to the country. The manager sent this young cowboy out to Blue Door Meadow, where Jiggs was staying alone in a cow camp cabin, many miles from the headquarters. The cowboy found the cabin and moved in with Jiggs.

 They went to bed that first night in two small cots set parallel in a small wing of the cabin. Jiggs bedded down facing this young cowboy, who knew nothing about the glass eye. He noticed soon after lying down that Jiggs seemed to be asleep but was looking at him with one eye. Eventually, he knew Jiggs was asleep, but the eye never closed. This unnerved the younger man. He didn't like that eye watching him all night. It bothered him so much that he got up and moved his own cot around the corner so he couldn't see the staring eye. But he still couldn't go to sleep and, every few minutes, got out of bed and peeked around to see if he was still being watched. Of course he was. The next morning he saddled up, rode the 35 miles back to the headquarters, quit, and left. No one ever told him about Jiggs's condition. As far as I know, he never figured it out.

Eddie and Walter, our two most reliable Native men, took my pickup one day to repair a corral fence up at the calving barn. They loaded some poles in the back, and away they went. The poles were too long for the bed of the pickup and teeter-tottered as they hung over the open tailgate. When they backed into the corral, one of the poles caught the ground and drove the other end through the rear window of the pickup.

They really felt bad about the misfortune. The next morning when I went outside, there was an intact (if not new) rear window lying at the back door. Later, in

Eddie Rosette

Walter Rosette at bear kill

the cook house, I thanked them for the window, mentioning that I had noticed that even though it had snowed that night there was no snow on the window. (Apparently when the window was put there it must have been warm enough to melt snow.) I also asked whether there were any places I shouldn't visit for a while. They both grinned and said it would probably be best not to go to Dog Creek for a few days. They said there was probably someone driving around Dog Creek with a very cold neck.

At Empire we actually had very few problems with theft, maybe because of what happened in an early encounter I had with the most prolific car thief in the area.

We were coming home one snowy day when I noticed vehicle tracks going up a draw. My curiosity aroused, I followed the tracks up this very narrow gully. Rounding a corner, I came on three or four Native fellows around a car that had been rolled over on its top. They were busily removing every part they could. Of course they were startled and very apprehensive about being discovered. I looked at the leader and told him that I would forget everything I was seeing, but there had better not be anything missing from Empire from then on. He agreed that might be a workable solution, and we never had a problem with theft. Several years later he told me that during that winter he had stolen 27 cars from Kamloops. He did spend some time in jail (or, as his kids told me, "working for the government").

Of course all the profit from stolen cars was in the parts. But they didn't hesitate to "acquire" a vehicle even if they lacked a ready market for it. One time they "borrowed" a U-Haul truck because it was left running somewhere and the temptation was just too strong. They drove this truck back to the reserve, but it was hard to hide; the box was visible above the bushes. So they used a chainsaw to cut the top of the box off. Problem solved.

Another time someone picked up a Coke delivery truck that was left running behind a store. The whole reserve had pop for a week.

(Another favorite trick was to go into a house right after someone had moved out and use the phone for long-distance calls. One time after we had moved to Oregon, someone from Dog Creek called Connie and talked nearly three hours. We had time to sort the purebreds and drive them across the valley and ride back before she got off the phone. A few weeks later, BC Tel called us in a futile attempt to locate the user of the B.C. phone.)

**Connie and boys cleaning Poison camp**

We spent each summer at Empire in the mountains with the cows. Each cowboy camp had a one-room line cabin with several cowboys. My wife wanted a little more privacy than such an arrangement afforded, so we usually lived in a camper on a 4x4 pickup. We used 12v for lights and propane for the fridge,

Tom & Theron with Connie's mom at Relay camp in Empire back country

given that we were at least an hour from a gasoline supply and three hours from a propane provider. The place we stayed the most was called Relay. We didn't have a travel trailer there; only a 4x4 could get there. A couple of times we almost had to resort to packing in gas for the truck by horseback. But we managed to avoid that unwelcome chore.

Hunters, and other kinds of visitors, sometimes camped in those mountains. Often one of these campers would post a simple sign pointing the way for others in his party. We often came on these signs. One of the Native cowboys' favorite tricks was to switch the signs, sending people the opposite direction. Several times, some poor gal who was supposed to be following the signs to their prospective camping spot would show up at our camp after hours of driving, totally lost the whole time because of the switched signs. After telling us her sad story and predicament, we knew just what had happened. I couldn't help those poor ladies because I usually wasn't with the guys when they had the bright idea of turning the signs. The cowboys certainly wouldn't help. In fact, after they had turned three or four signs around, even they lost track of the original directions. Usually I just drew the poor, lost soul a map of how to get back to town and left it at that. The problem was that much of the country had logging roads crisscrossing it, and the roads all looked alike anyway.

Connie and Tristan at Poison cowboy cabin

Tom and sons at Poison cabin

## FIRST NATIONS

The Native guys had a real hatred for signs. Closer to the headquarters, the issue was highway signs put out by the B.C. Highways people. These took a little more work, as they had to be dug up and then turned or moved.

One fall, the highway people had installed a lot of new signs along the roads giving directions, distances, etc. I was happy, because outsiders such as repairmen, truckers, and friends really needed the signs to find us. My happiness didn't last long, though, as over a few days the signs all disappeared.

That winter I went with one of our Native employees to see about a repair he wanted us to do on his house. When we got behind the house, out of sight to passersby, I discovered a whole pile of highway signs, complete with the wooden posts. There was evidence that the posts were being cut up and used as firewood. I glanced over at the employee and he just gave me his great big toothless grin. Nothing was ever mentioned again about the signs.

Nobody I know likes to be awakened in the middle of the night to face some major problem. Life at Empire, or almost anywhere in the Chilcotin, adds another dimension to such an experience. When you are the responsible person on a ranch with several people living there, you have to become sheriff, judge, sewer plumber, counselor, bouncer, arbitrator, and all-around fool. It takes a sense of humor more than anything, because if you ain't laughing you're crying.

At about two o'clock one morning, my wife and I were awakened from a sound, peaceful sleep by a voice that sounded like it was right beside our bed: "Phyllis's water broke!" We both sat straight up in bed in a split-second without coming anywhere near consciousness. I turned to my wife, still in a stupor, and said, "It's summer, water don't broke in summer." The voice repeated, "Phyllis's water broke." Finally, we woke up, jumped out of bed, and headed downstairs to see what was happening. Dave Lush had been sleeping downstairs when he was awakened by frantic knocking on the back door. Someone was in a state of panic and yelled at him just what he had relayed to us. We decided that this could be serious and we had better go down to the house where the pregnant girl lived. I said, as my wife rushed out the door, "She's not a first-calfer so you won't need the puller and the chains." She said, sarcastically, "I sure hope not."

When she arrived down at the employees' house she soon observed that the girl really did need to get to a doctor or hospital VERY soon. They had left me at our house to try to arrange for an ambulance and some EMTs to head out our way and tell them we would meet them. (Of course in these situations we always took pains to identify the right road; we didn't want them coming out one road while the maternity party was going in on another.) The emergency was complicated by the fact that the phone happened to be out of order, so I had to use the radio phone.

My wife came back to get all the towels in the house for the ride into town. We parted knowing that she was in for a miserable ride. The week before, the driver had been working on this old car, a beat-up station wagon, and took it for a test drive. He crossed a cattle guard going a little too fast. When the car leaped over the guard and landed, the motor jumped up and turned partially sideways. He had forgotten to tie the motor down. All this didn't reassure us about the trip my wife was about to take. We offered our 4x4, but the driver said he was more familiar with his car.

They put the girl in the back seat and threw gravel everywhere as they took off for town. My wife was riding in the front seat next to the driver, on her knees leaning over the seat to help the girl, who was moaning loudly and screaming occasionally. Each scream prodded the driver to go even faster. The car bounced off both banks several times as they sped on to meet the ambulance, or their fate, whichever came first.

After an hour at this pace they spotted the ambulance and slid to a stop. The EMTs hurriedly loaded the girl into the ambulance and headed back to Williams Lake. After my wife got home, she said it really was good that she had been facing backwards, or she might have panicked watching the winding road ahead.

The girl didn't give birth until later that day, so everything ended well. My wife, however, came home and dropped in total exhaustion.

Believe it or not, the same thing happened a year or so later, except this time it was winter and the roads were very icy. The driver raced at breakneck speed again, sliding around the corners. My wife knew not to look ahead to see where they were sure to die. On this occasion, the delivery time came sooner. They met the EMTs and the baby came as they were lifting the mother into the ambulance. That was too close.

From then on, I begged the pregnant one to go to town and stay until the delivery. Of course they totally ignored me, as usual. I finally got smart and decided to stand a calf puller, complete with chains and a cable saw, by their front door. This seemed to speak louder than all the pleading that had gone on before. I received quite a few dirty looks, but it was worth it, and I just grinned real wide.

Empire was 80 miles from the paved highway. Almost every time we went to town, once a month or less, we would see something interesting along the road. But this story was told to us by a neighbor. He witnessed the following account one day when he was swathing hay in a field along the road to Gang Ranch and Empire.

An old car was coming along the road when it slowed and stopped. The occupants, several Native people, got out, raised the hood, and worked under there for a while. Soon, apparently satisfied about the repairs, they all got back in and prepared for departure. But the cussed thing wouldn't start. The battery must have been dead. Four or five young men were in the group, so pushing would not have been a problem, except that the car had stalled in the bottom of a dip in the road, making pushing by the occupants impossible. Especially occupants as intoxicated as these.

A lengthy and sometimes heated discussion ensued about the best course of action. Finally they hit on an idea all could agree on and immediately put the plan into action. Some old poles were lying along the road next to the fence. They used these as levers to raise one rear wheel of the car off the ground. When the wheel was four or five inches in the air they produced a lariat rope from the trunk which they wound around the tire several times, leaving about ten feet to hold. If they could pull the rope with enough speed and force, the car should start. First they had to decide which one would be assigned the task of holding the clutch down until just the right moment before engaging it to start the engine. Basically, the decision was simple: whoever was too drunk to pull on the rope would be the designated driver. They "gently" placed the most inebriated individual behind the steering wheel with loud, adamant, and no doubt confusing instructions.

The other four positioned themselves along the rope and prepared to run with the end of the rope and spin the tire. (The fact that they wound the rope in the right direction suggested this may not have been the first time they had employed this ingenuity.) The clutch was depressed, the four took off at high speed and the wheel spun beautifully. All went well except the driver forgot to let the clutch out and as the end of the rope unwound from the tire, the four all fell in a heap. While some rewound the tire, the others dragged the driver out and gave him a tuneup to help him remember to let the clutch out next time.

The driver was not about to make the same mistake again, so on the next pull he let the clutch out almost immediately. The four pullers had not achieved enough momentum to keep the wheel spinning, and this time were jerked to the ground in the opposite direction from the first pile-up. Again, while some rewound the tire, the others facilitated another training session with the poor driver. After two or three more failed attempts, it finally all came together, more by accident than design, and the engine started. They lowered the car to the road, piled back in with a new driver at the wheel, and raced on to their destination.

"She's no more good!" That diagnosis of a broken-down vehicle was one of the most common remarks we heard in our area. Few late-model vehicles frequented our roads. In a remote area with poor roads and mostly old cars and trucks, you see some pretty amazing and ingenious methods of vehicle maintenance.

One day, on the way to meet the mail stage, I came upon several young Natives I didn't recognize, all sitting in a circle on a blanket on the ground beside their incapacitated vehicle. It was 100 degrees and they had a good-sized fire going. When I stopped and got out, I saw that they had a lot of small, oily parts spread out on the blanket. Soon I could see that they had their automatic transmission in pieces on the blanket. From what I could see I would say that the seals were "no more good." In that remote setting, they were replacing the seals by melting the pitch in a log and then applying the pitch to the parts needing seals. The fire, which they had built to melt the pitch in the log, was what had attracted my attention; it was unusual to see people huddled around a fire on a hot summer day. Later in the day I came back by that point on my way home, and they were gone. I hadn't met them on the road, either, so the repair must have worked, for a while at least.

# FIRST NATIONS

The local hippie had an old Ford that had seen better days and was pretty rusted out. You could watch the road through a hole in the floorboard right in front of each rear wheel. In the winter, when the roads were slick, he would have been much better (especially given his personality) just to stay home. But that wasn't what he wanted. He wanted to travel, and the car's condition actually provided an ingenious method to supply traction on the slick roads. He filled several five gallon pails with sand and set them in the back where the seat had been. When he started to spin climbing a hill, he reached in the back into a bucket, grabbed some sand and trickled it out on the road through the rust hole, just ahead of his rear tire. This worked really well for climbing. Descending those steep hills presented a different problem. Even when his brakes were good enough to slow him sufficiently (which wasn't always the case), he still had the traction problem. Again, he hit on an interesting solution. He started carrying an axe and some pieces of chain in the trunk. Whenever he was approaching a steep downgrade he would stop and use the axe to cut down a sizable tree, chain it to the back of his car, and drag it to the bottom of the hill. During a snowy, slick winter we would find several abandoned logs near the suspension bridge.

One fall when I was hauling cattle to Kamloops and traveling the road every day, I saw a very nice, fairly new van parked by the river, with no one around. I found out later that some rafters had left it there to use when they arrived at the end of their river trip. They had gone about 150 miles up the Fraser to put in their rafts and float back down to the van. To them, it seemed like a great idea. What could go wrong? But as soon as I saw it, I knew if it was not occupied or moved soon it was in grave danger.

My suspicions were soon confirmed. The first day the van was just parked there, locked and presumably safe. The second day, the van had seemed to shrink into the ground. On closer inspection I saw that the tires and wheels were gone and it was sitting on the axles and frame. The third day the doors were all open, the seats and radio gone, as well as anything else removable. The fourth day, the grill had been beaten out with a sledge hammer and the motor and transmission dragged out through the front. The last day, the van body was upside-down and all the axles, brakes, and other fine parts were missing. That's what the rafters found when they pulled out of the river, 60 miles from town and at least 15 miles from the nearest phone.[9]

My experience in the region suggests how the rest of the story went: The van strippers used the parts to immediately rebuild another van, which they drove to the river. There, they offered the distressed rafters a ride to town in a van rebuilt from their own parts. And the perpetrators had a big laugh at those "dumb rafters."

Any time the Natives could pull one over on an unsuspecting white man, they got a big kick out of it. The people at Dog Creek felt pretty much toward our resident hippie as we did, which led to a special offer they made him. They sold him some ducks that were fat and ready for eating. After the purchase, the Natives told me those ducks had been raised in the sewer outlet for the Dog Creek Reserve. They thought this was extremely funny and referred to them as Ron's poop ducks. Actually, everyone in the area loved this story, but Ron never figured it out.

That story reminds me of a scene I witnessed one time out on the Chilcotin Plateau. I was driving through a small reserve (maybe Toosie) near Riske Creek. A few cabins were situated along the creek. About 100 feet from the road was the community outhouse, built on stilts right over the creek. The building was dead center over the creek. A railed plank walkway led out to the building for safety in icy conditions.

I have thought many times how effective that design was. No cleaning, no redigging, and no odor. The only maintenance required was making sure the stilts didn't rot. Of course, it may have been a little brisk at 40 below, especially with a bit of a breeze going down the creek. One of the things that I most enjoyed about this scene is just what it must have meant to the environmentalists driving by.

Eddie was one of the best. He was a young man from one of the local reserves who showed up one day and stayed 12 years. Eddie didn't ride at all, but he was good at whatever he did. He was in charge of the irrigation and ran machinery most of the time. He was careful, a pretty good mechanic, but most memorable was his great sense of humor and his ability to see humor in ordinary things. Much of my understanding

---

[9] Of course this was before cellphone service, but even today these roads are generally beyond cell coverage.

of the workings of the local Shuswap culture came from my closeness to Eddie and his willingness to share his observations with me.

One afternoon I went into the shop to see how Eddie was coming on a repair job and found him in the back of the shop with one eye glued to a knothole in the wooden siding. I could see that whatever he was watching had him highly agitated: he kept his eye inserted in the hole, but in the meantime, his feet were trying to run. I wanted to understand this strange behavior, so I asked him if he minded me looking. He reluctantly moved aside, and I inserted an eye. At first I couldn't see anything unusual, just a couple of the ranch houses. Finally, after looking more closely, I saw the reason for his agitation. An RCMP vehicle was parked in front of Eddie's house. He almost knocked me out of the way so he could look again. He kept telling himself they were surely after him and that he had better run. He was just about ready to make a run for it.

I suggested maybe we should figure something out, because I didn't think running would be a very good idea. I asked him what was going on. He figured it was probably related to a burglary at the Gang Ranch shop the night before. I knew he wasn't in on the burglary, because that was not Eddie's way of living and I was pretty sure he had been home all night. (Stealing one of the wives of the RCMP officers, however, that would be a different story. I couldn't have vouched for his innocence in a case like that.)

He really wanted to run, so I asked him why they were coming to talk to him and what he knew. He said they weren't coming there just to talk to him; he was pretty sure that his sister's boyfriend had done the job. In that culture, it was much safer to take your chances with the RCMP than to rat on someone. We didn't have much time to prepare for their visit, but I told him to go out and meet the officers and not let them find him hiding in the shop. He fervently did not want to do this, but I leaned on him to go to them, answer their questions, but don't offer any information that wasn't asked for. I also suggested that if possible he should try to stop shaking all over and get his feet to quit dancing as if they were ready to head for higher ground.

First he went back to the hole. As soon as he looked, he jumped at least two feet in the air and almost shouted that they were coming to the shop. When they pulled up in front of the shop I told him once more what to do and that if things didn't go well I would do whatever I could to help him. He went out to meet the officers and was very cooperative in every way, but without offering answers to questions they didn't ask. It went very well and they left. When they were out of sight, Eddie very nearly collapsed and came back into the shop, where he started the shakes again. I told him to go home and try to relax the rest of the day and maybe by tomorrow he would be well again. I really believe that his friendliness and cooperation so shocked the officers that they never got around to asking him anything that could have caused him trouble.

Often, after the Williams Lake Stampede or some other festivities, the crew would come home with numerous injuries of various sorts, everything from really bad human bites to nearly missing ears. Eddie, however, always came home without a single small scratch. After several times of this, I asked him why he escaped the injuries. He just smiled really big and said that he just wasn't a fighter, because he really preferred being a lover. After seeing some of his girlfriends I could sure see his point. His taste in girlfriends was phenomenal, and he sure could find the best lookers by a long way.

Often an officer from the RCMP would stop at the ranch and ask if we had seen some Native individual. One young officer said that the man he was looking for was dark complected, about 150 pounds, five-foot-eight and Native. As he said, "Now, who in the world out here doesn't fit that description?"

I worked for a man many years ago who had been a Mountie and had been sent after a wanted individual in northern Alberta. As he was preparing for the long horse-pack trip, he hired a Native guide to show him the way and do some translation. They spent several months travelling to numerous villages inquiring after the wanted man's whereabouts, but no one seemed to know anything about it. Finally they were sent to an old chief who would surely know the man they were after. When they found the chief and asked him, he said, "You brought him with you," pointing at his guide. Monty, the RCMP officer, was devastated and asked his guide why he hadn't told him who he was. The guide replied that Monty had never asked him. When Monty relayed the story to his superiors, he admitted the hardest part was informing them that the RCMP owed the wanted man two months of wages for looking for himself. Monty's story is told in a book titled North to Adventure. He was noted for being the first RCMP officer to make it to the North Pole. That adventure involved two years of living in igloos and traveling with dogsleds. The trip didn't take as long as one might expect, but the entrance to Baffin Bay never thawed out the next summer, so the ship that was to pick them up was delayed for a year. When he returned to his home town they had erected a statue of him, as they thought he had been lost in the north.

## CHAPTER EIGHT

# WILDLIFE

We ate a lot of wild game over the years at Empire. Especially salmon. From late June through the end of July, the Native people on the ranch would go down to the Fraser River every night and dip-net the salmon, which were running up the river. Their method of fishing was as important a cultural tradition as was the actual catching of the fish. They would build a big bonfire and have a great time. The designated fisherman would tie a rope around his waist with the other end secured to a very large rock up the bank. He took his stand on a boulder that stuck out in the river, where the water moved faster as it flowed around the rock. He would dip the net into the river and move it with the current, an action which precluded using a conventional net because the flow of the water would push the soft netting through the hoop. Chicken wire was the best material, as it was stiff enough to hold its shape. (Early in our time at Empire we wondered why our chickens were always getting out every year at the beginning of the salmon run. When we figured it out, we started buying a roll of new chicken wire just before the run and then laying the roll of wire right where the old wire had gone missing the year before. They furnished us with so much wonderful salmon that we were happy to contribute to the program.)

They could catch and use all the salmon they wanted, but they were forbidden by law from selling or even giving any away. However, they gave us lots, and we really appreciated it. They brought so much to our door that by July we were beginning to look forward to the end of the run. It is a real insult to turn down anything they offer as a gift,[10] so we were saturated and probably smelled very fishy for a month.

---

[10] This obligation to accept a gift took on a whole new meaning when one of the girls who was close to my wife became pregnant and told my wife she was going to give her the baby. You can imagine how much this offer was discussed around our dinner table and often late into the night. When the birth came, the girl was busy and must have forgotten her earlier statement. After several months we relaxed a bit.

# WILDLIFE

One of our employees really liked selling fish. Every night, after he had made his catch he would throw the fish into the trunk of his car and head for town to sell them. Needless to say, over time his car began to smell. In the heat of July it began to reek. He complained a lot about all the dogs following him every time he drove through the reserve. Several times he filled the trunk with water and added soap, but to no avail. He even added a couple of bottles of his girlfriend's perfume, but that only gave it a horrible sweet smell (and ruined any effect the perfume might have had on the girl). In the end, he had to abandon the car and wait until winter to strip all its useable parts.

Every year in the early spring, suckers would come up to spawn in a fairly large, spring-fed lake. They would come out from under three feet of ice to spawn, and then die. The bald eagles and coyotes would

Suckers spawning in spring-fed lake at Empire

Suckers

come for the feast, lined up along the edge of the ice much like cattle at a feedlot bunk. The ice would literally turn red from the fish blood. The eagles and coyotes would be all mixed together and seemed to get along fine.

Next to salmon in abundance was venison, of which we also ate a lot. Empire was famous for its deer herds, so we could stock up during the season and the venison would last some time.

Next was blue grouse. These were especially helpful around the cow camps, where we had no refrigeration. Unlike most meats, they could be consumed before they spoiled. Our boys also spent nearly every afternoon after school hunting grouse. Our younger son would go out every day with his BB gun and wouldn't say where he was going. We never thought much about it, until one day when he returned to the house with a very large grouse. It gave him great pride to have taken a grouse with a BB gun.

Last was trout. We could catch them any time, but they were only good to eat in the early spring, before the hot weather came, and in the fall after it had left. In the summer the lakes were so shallow the fish got very soft and weren't fit to eat. The best ones were those caught near the end of their prime from a high mountain lake. The trout in the streams were firm all summer, but the streams were glacier-fed so the water was a gray color. The fish were okay, but not really good.

The one exception to this was a lake called Gaspard that was big enough and deep enough that the fish from there were always good. There were so many fish in the stream just below the dam that you couldn't cast a fly without catching a fish. They were small but delicious. There was a Gang Ranch cow camp near there, and the cowboys had an effective method of catching the trout. The outlet water from the dam spilled out of a culvert. They would set a bucket at the edge of the waterfall so that, as the trout tried to go up the waterfall, many would be flipped back and land in the bucket. This was a very simple and reliable way of getting supper. I was there lots of times, and always the bucket would be full of delicious trout.

Tom's bear kill (and infamous hat)

We did not eat bear, as I had tried it once in Colorado when I was young and didn't like it at all. In fact, when we tried to give bear meat to the dogs the hair came up on their backs and they growled and wouldn't touch it. Of course, the flavor of bear meat depends on what the animal has been eating. Even the experience of skinning a bear can be very different depending on its diet. A bear that has just consumed a rotten old cow isn't prime eating, to say the least. If you must eat bear, probably the best time is after the wild berries come on.

Moose and bighorn sheep were really great, but we seldom got them. The moose were scarce and the sheep were generally very hard to hunt for trophies, let alone just for meat. The Natives got both and relished the moose.

The one place we often saw sheep (but not during the hunting season) was in Churn Creek canyon. The canyon and the hills on both sides are home to a fantastic band of bighorn sheep. I once saw five of the biggest rams ever at this canyon. All were 1¼ to 1½ curl and absolutely beautiful. That was in late November and they weren't real wild. The local guide said that they were only wild from late July through the middle of November. I know he was correct because he and I rode right in among a band of about 20 in May when we were hunting a grizzly. They were no wilder than cattle at that time. My wife went for a walk through this same area a few days later and walked right up on the same band. She and the boys stood for a long time and watched them graze and the lambs play. She even saw some of the lambs jump up and stand on their mother's back.

On a flat near Churn Creek I saw bighorn sheep digging the grass out of the snow and then our steers taking it away from them. Also down there I witnessed bighorn sheep and cattle licking the same salt block at the same time. In the same spot I saw my first wolf track in the snow.

We had lots of eagles at Empire Valley, both bald and golden. I have counted as many as 71 bald eagles around one of our lakes at one time.

The road to Empire crossed a hill called Eagle Tree. Here's the story behind the site. One spring, when the eagles were especially bad, the Native cowboys killed a dozen and hung them in a tree right beside the road. Eventually the game warden came by and, of course, he was somewhat concerned. He saw some of the Native cowboys nearby and made an attempt to arrest them. They told him, somewhat forcefully, that if he didn't shut up and leave he would be hanging in that tree in the middle of those eagles. That ended the conversation and he left.

The bald eagles are natural fish eaters, so they were less likely to kill calves than were the golden eagles, who were vicious on calves. Both ate fish, however, and we were forced to delay calving until this alternate feed source became available to help lure the eagles away from the calves being born. Their method of killing calves was grisly but effective. They watched for a cow to start calving. When the newborn was started out, before the cow could get up, the eagle would fly down and peck the eyes out of the calf. They would then return to the top of a nearby tree and wait. After giving birth, the cow would try to rouse the calf. When she finally gave up and left, the eagles would proceed to dine.

Every year we would find several calves that had been picked up by an eagle, only to be dropped when they proved too heavy. The attempt often occurred when the calf was a day or two old. Typically, the calf would recover, with scars and a humped back. They were easy to spot in the bunch. Eagle wounds, as well as cougar wounds, could be doctored with some success. Wounds from bear attacks, on the other hand, would never heal and the animal would eventually die.

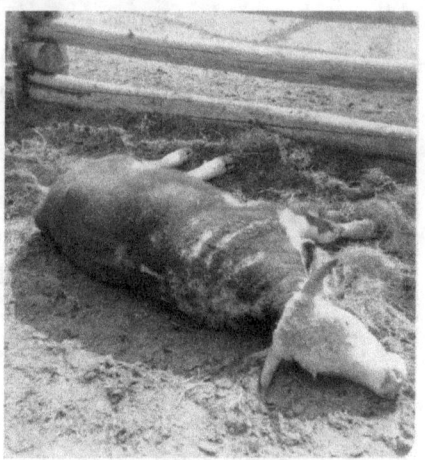

Empire heifer wounded by cougar

Lamb seemed to be the favorite dinner for the golden eagles, so we delayed our calving until the bighorn sheep were lambing, as that would take the golden eagles out of the picture for a while. A bird would wait until a lamb was crossing a high, treacherous cliff and then dive-bomb the lamb and knock it off the ledge onto the rocks far below.

One time, at Big Bar, along the Fraser, a golden eagle picked up a toddler playing in his front yard. The bird was just able to lift the little boy off the ground, and started carrying him to a cliff several hundred feet away to drop him over. Thankfully, an older child saw what was happening and grabbed his little brother's pants with one hand and a saw horse with the other. He screamed for help and hung on for dear

## WILDLIFE

life until the mother arrived with a broom. Finally the eagle dropped the child and left.

Bears were an everyday phenomenon at Empire. When they weren't hibernating, we had them everywhere. We didn't have a lot of entertainment—no TV and few social activities—so hunting bears became our favorite and most frequently enjoyed pastime. The bears always took a toll on our cattle, so it was mandatory that we get rid of offenders. We enjoyed the hunting and needed to eliminate the cattle killers, so it was a double bonus for us.

We took an unusually colored black bear off a dead horse bait one time. But the real story had nothing to do with the bear's color.

Yodel camp, Empire back country

We were near our main line cow camp called Yodel. Our Native cow foreman and my boys and I were sitting behind an old log about

150 yards up a hill from the bait. We were actually hoping for a grizzly who was in the area, but this bear came along instead. After I shot him we took a rope to drag him away from the bait so his carcass wouldn't spook other bears; we were especially eager to get the grizzly. He was a pretty bear just out of hibernation, so we took his picture. Then we dragged him some distance to a steep bank above the old creek channel and tossed him over the 12-foot drop.

We proceeded back up to our lookout to wait for other visitors. The only thing that came that evening was one very skittish coyote. He was also very curious. When we first noticed him he was sitting just inside the trees, watching the bait. He then proceeded to move completely around the bait, always sitting down and watching just inside the tree line. Finally, his curiosity got the best of him and he approached the horse with GREAT caution. As he got nearer the bait, he smelled our tracks and those of the bear, and he sniffed everywhere to see who had been there and just what had happened. He kept stopping and cautiously looking around. Several times he spooked himself and raced off into the trees, but his curiosity always got the best of him and he came back to his investigation. Finally he discovered the track where we had dragged the bear, and that immediately got his interest. He followed the trail by crisscrossing it many times, trying to figure which way we had gone dragging the bear. He finally settled on the right track, working his way toward the bank where we had dumped the bear. Of course he couldn't see the dead bear, so he worked his way right up to the edge of the sharp bank and looked over. Now the bear was right under his nose. When he discovered the bear, I'll swear he jumped straight up in the air at least four feet and when he landed, he was already running at top speed and never stopped. It was as if he said, "THERE HE IS, JUST WHAT I FEARED!"

We were all laughing so hard we wouldn't have been able to shoot the grizzly even if he had shown up. However, the presence of a grizzly can be pretty sobering, and we might have sharpened up real quick.

Some of the bear stories were funny, others were sad.

One day, while driving through Gang Ranch, we were passing Bear Spring Meadow. It was evening but still light. A beekeeper had put out quite a few hives that were visible from the road. As we passed the beehives we saw a young bear up on a hive. He was using his front claws to try to pull off the top of the hive. He was having trouble because he was standing on the lid he was trying to lift. We nearly died laughing at the antics of this young bear.

A tragic and maddening story happened one night at Yodel. Two Native cowboys were awakened in the middle of the night by the most awful noise they had ever heard. The sound was somewhat muffled, but clearly some animal, they could not identify what, was in agony and panic. It had them genuinely spooked. They couldn't go back to bed and at the same time were too scared to investigate in the dark. They stayed up, built a fire in the stove, and made some coffee. Actually, they drank several pots of coffee. Eventually they ran out of water but were terrified about going down to the creek for more. Finally the older man got brave enough to head out with a bucket. When he was almost at the creek he heard a noise behind him. He spun around to hightail it for the cabin and ran smack into the younger cowboy. He had decided he didn't like being alone in the cabin and had fetched his gun and followed the other man. They both hit the dirt and scrambled, in a panic, to get to their feet. The younger one explained why he had followed, admitting he had been afraid. After they calmed down some, they talked themselves into getting the water and heading back.

The horrible noise continued all night. At first light they saddled up and headed toward it, eager as well as terrified to know what was happening. They soon came on a terrible scene. A black bear had knocked a cow down and broken her back so she couldn't move, but she hadn't died. She was partly submerged in the creek and was bawling in terror and pain as the bear was eating her alive. Her entire hindquarters was nearly gone.

The cowboys shot the bear and then the cow, but even after the bear was dead they couldn't quit shooting him. When they finally ran out of bullets they headed out for the three-hour ride to a mine telephone to call me. They told me the story and added that they needed more bullets. And, oh yes, they were out of coffee, too.

I headed out for the camp with several boxes of ammunition and more coffee, decaf this time. When I got to the camp they were still bouncing around and chattering in a high pitch.

You need a sense of humor to live with bears all around. Otherwise, they can make your life miserable. The following story is one of the more humorous and yet potentially disastrous.

In his younger days, our neighbor and good friend, Jack, was an excellent roper and liked to practice on anything that came across his path. One day he and a Native man were riding to check the cattle when they came across a medium-sized bear out in the open, where a good chase would be possible. He was on his best roping horse, so he shook out his rope and went after the bear. The horse was very fast and the bear got a late start, so Jack easily caught up to within roping distance and threw. The rope went neatly over the bear's head, but before it tightened, the bear, without breaking stride, reached up and swatted it off of his neck.

So far, so good, for the bear at least. But then the rope tightened around his foot instead!

Just as the rope was going over the bear's head, Jack thought, "Something here is not right." When the rope tightened around the bear's leg he immediately turned around and started back towards Jack. Then it hit Jack just what wasn't quite right. He had roped a grizzly, not a black bear, as he had thought. This simple fact brought a whole new dimension to the saga.

Jack was without his rifle. He hadn't wanted to carry the rifle on this, his favorite horse, so he had given it to the Native man to carry. Jack and his horse spun around and headed back toward the man carrying the gun, with the grizzly in hot pursuit. As he went by the armed man and started circling around him, he yelled for the man to shoot the bear, now very close behind and gaining.

The Native man yelled back, "I can't hit a running bear! You'll have to stop!" Jack then yelled, "I CAN'T STOP. Just SHOOT the bear." This desperate circus continued until, finally, the man shot, hit the bear, and everyone breathed a sigh of relief. Especially Jack.

One summer day, one of our irrigators was up in a meadow about three miles above the house, moving some irrigation wheel lines. The upper end line ran up to some chokecherry bushes along an old creek bed. When he was working on that line, an older bear bounced kind of stiff-legged out of the bushes right toward him, woofing as she came. Spooked somewhat, he raced back to the trail bike, piled on with great speed and started kicking the starter pedal. The bike refused to start, but after frantically kicking it for some time he realized he hadn't turned the ignition key on. As soon as he did, the bike started, and he left the bear in a cloud of dust. He told us later that he had been kicking the bike so fast he figured it was turning over at least 2,000 rpm when he finally discovered the ignition problem.

Later in the year, our older son was up there moving that same line when the bear bounced out and woofed at him. He tried his bike but it would not start (even with the key on!) and he had to run quite a ways. After he had gone about a mile he was able to catch a horse and ride home using bale twine for a bridle. When he told his mom the story, she immediately decided to go after that bear and end this nonsense. I was in the back country hunting grizzlies, so she felt she had to do it alone. She took my lighter rifle and headed out with our boys in the pickup. When she got up to the meadow, the bear was crossing in the open and heading up a steep hillside. She jumped out, grabbed the .25-06, told the boys to be ready to reload for her, and started shooting. The bear was about 300 to 400 yards away; she hadn't wanted to get too close. I think she emptied the gun twice and, although none of the three bears dropped, she was pretty sure she had hit at least one. It was a momma bear (the woofer) with two cubs, her yearling and a cub born that spring. I got home later that night and she insisted that we go back up there in the morning to see if she had hit any of the bears.

When we got to the meadow, we ran into the yearling and prepared to take it. She had started this hunt and wanted to finish it, so we let her have the first shot. It was moving, and her first round creased it on the rear quarters. The bear sat down and started scooting along in a sitting position, like a dog does sometimes. Quickly, she shot again and downed it.

Later we found the sow dead very near where she had been shot at the day before, and the cub, also dead, not far from

Connie at bear kill

there. My wife was quite proud of herself for her shooting and bear hunting.

One year when we had an early spring at Empire, we were moving our calved-out two-year-old heifers to a small pasture and corral setup that was called the "calving barn." It was about three miles from the house, so we didn't use it for calving heifers, because no one wanted to stay up there in a rat-infested barn when his house was only three miles away. We put the heifers there in the small pasture with the gates open to the range, so they could mother up well before going out.

Several of the workers mentioned they had seen a bear hanging around that little pasture, playing with the calves. We figured that was one habit we didn't want to encourage. So every evening, my family and I would drive up there and see if we could spot the bear in his antics. One evening we spotted him walking along the road just above the cattle. He was some distance off, and we didn't want to spook him until we had a chance for a shot. He turned and started off the edge of the road, and I broke a rule I have always had: Don't shoot until you are absolutely sure you are going to hit and kill. I mistakenly took a quick shot as he disappeared over the bank. We were pretty sure the bullet had hit, but we didn't know where. We drove up to the spot where he had been, and sure enough there was blood, but no bear. There was a fairly large patch of chokecherries at the bottom of the hill that we figured he had probably gone into. But there was no noise or sign of the bear in the bushes.

My wife suggested that I should go down into those bushes and see what had happened to him. It was nearly dark by then, and the prospect of crawling through those thick bushes was not all that appealing. Besides, we only had one gun and we were having trouble deciding just who was going to have it. She thought that I should leave the gun with her, and then she could shoot whatever was chasing me out of the bushes. I argued that this might not be the best plan, as the bear might get to me before I could get to where she could shoot at least one of us (exactly which one would depend on how close the bear was and how much she let him!). I was able to keep discussion going until it really was dark, and we headed home.

Later, in the fall of that year, we began to notice a very unusual track of a bear that had three normal footprints but one very rounded and odd-shaped track. We figured that this was the bear I had hit earlier in the year. The next spring, one of the riders saw a bear in that same area that was missing a major part of his right rear leg, and we were sure that was the bear. He lived for several years in that condition, but we were never able to get another shot at him. We saw his tracks for several years and then one year they just disappeared, so he must have passed on.

At least one bear story features a much smaller mammal. One fall we were hunting grizzlies: the whole family, plus one Native man was staying at our Yodel cow camp. The first night, my wife slept on a cot along the west wall of the cabin, which turned out to be right over an entrance a rat had been using. We didn't hear him come in, but after he was in, he stopped and sneezed real loud. I'd swear that my wife was still in the prone position when she lifted up off of her cot several inches. She was unable to sleep much that night, but the next night we assured her that he surely would have cured his cold by now and she would be okay. Right after we were starting to doze off, he came in and stopped and sneezed again several times. She repeated the prior night's performance, but this time she got up and moved her sleeping bag to the top of the table where we ate. It was great, high, rat-proof and quite large. For many years afterward, this table became her permanent bed every night we stayed there. We named the rat "Sneezer," and we tried everything to rid ourselves of him, lest we catch his cold.

When our youngest son was small, a rat took up residence under the back end of our bathtub. He came in from outside and was sealed off there from being able to enter the house. Whenever he entered or exited his nest, he always bumped his head on the bottom of the tub, a bump you could feel if you happened to be in the tub. This drove our son nuts, and he went into some kind of fit every time. Upon quizzing him, we finally understood his fears: what if the rat crawled out of the tub faucet? Did you ever try explaining plumbing to a four-year-old?

I was staying at the Yodel cabin one fall with Alec, our wonderful old cow foreman and guide. We were sleeping in the bunks. I had to have the top, as my feet always hung over. Alec was fine with the lower bunk because it was the most comfortable in the cabin. We had quite a mouse problem at the time, because the two cats we had put there in the spring had come to a disagreement with our cow dogs. The cats were so upset that they quit their jobs and headed for parts unknown, leaving us with a totally unnecessary surplus population of mice.

When we both were in bed and the cabin was dark, we could hear mice scurrying about. Since this was a rough-log cabin, the walls served as a system of mouse interstate highways. As one mouse raced past Alec he detoured into Alec's sleeping bag. Alec calmly said, "A mouse just went down inside my sleeping bag, and I can feel him crawling around my toes. Maybe I should get up and let him out of there." He had no sooner said that when he added, "That mouse is coming up and is leaving now." I can't imagine what my wife would have done if that had been her, but I assure you the scene would have been neither calm nor pretty.

Alec Rosette and faithful dog, Puppy

I have never understood how a woman so fearless with bears could go batty over a minuscule mouse.

Actually, over the years my wife has become quite an accomplished and noted mouse trapper. Her record is two mice side-by-side in one trap. I suggested that maybe we should have the whole thing mounted to hang beside our other trophies, but she declined that generous offer.

Three hunting guides worked in our area: Pete Coldwell from Jesmond, B.C., and Gordon Menhenick and Pat Girard from Gold Bridge, B.C. Each November they trailed their horses to Empire for us to winter on the top of Clyde Mountain. (The pack strings had picked that spot to winter many years ago. Most of those strings were made up of Clydesdale horses, which is how the mountain got its name.)

Pete wanted to trade a guided, one-week bear hunt for his pasture bill. I took him up on his offer and had a really great time with him on those hunts. He had hunted that territory for nearly 40 years and had a wealth of stories. These hunts were always in May, after snow had melted in the mountain trail passes. We would move from camp to camp and scout out the south-facing slopes where we might find an early spring growth of dandelions, a favorite bear food. We were really hunting for a grizzly but instead got lots of black bears. Often we would bait the bears by putting down an ancient pack horse and then waiting ten days for the bears to be drawn to the carcass. This worked well; we got most of the bears with this method. We had to chain the horse's leg to a tree, or a grizzly would move it where we couldn't see to shoot. Pete had seen a grizzly grab a 1,200-pound horse from the top of the shoulders and sling it over like turning a blanket, the entire horse in the air at one point. That really opened the eyes of the hunter he was guiding and made him very conscious of the need to shoot straight.

On one of these hunts, I rode through aspen groves in the Tyaughton Valley (a Native name, I was told, for "good little things from the ground") where a group of First Nations people were snowed in an entire winter one time and survived by digging up and eating groundhogs. In those aspen groves you could ride up to a tree and, still on the horse, reaching as high as you could, just touch the scratch marks of a large grizzly.

Pete told me about one of his hunters who had wounded a big grizzly, only to have the bear charge. The hunter was carrying a .375 magnum, but instead of firing again he threw the gun in the air and ran. Pete shot and killed the bear with a 12-gauge shotgun loaded with a slug, dropping the bear before he reached Pete. When the hunter stopped running and came back to the scene, he said to Pete, "Boy, oh boy, it sure is good nobody got excited, or someone could have been hurt!"

We tried to find one grizzly in particular, a bear that killed a cow every year just before he went into hibernation, sort of a midnight snack. He buried a cow in the same area every year and then hibernated, but when we got there in the spring the cow had long since been dug up and consumed.

One fall I was in the same area where this grizzly operated, driving a black baldie up a steep and narrow trail out of a canyon named Starvation. The cow showed signs of weed poisoning, as she was bleeding from the mouth. In a very steep spot on the trail she decided to stop, so I took the rest of the cattle on up to Yodel camp and started them towards home. The next morning I drove the two-hour trip home.

Later that day, I got a call from Pete. He said he and his sheep hunters and their pack string had been attacked by the grizzly right at the spot where I had left the cow. The bear had killed the cow and was eating her. It charged when Pete's party happened by. But for his little border collie, who distracted the bear while they made their escape, the story might have ended in tragedy. He had ridden two hours to a mine camp to call me, so I knew he was serious.

I left immediately and drove back to Yodel camp, where I saddled up and rode back to the site. When I got to the cow she had been completely consumed; only the hide remained. It was nearly dark, in a patch of tall spruce trees that created a cathedral effect. The hair was literally standing up on the back of my neck, but there was no sign of the bear, almost to my relief.

That grizzly had consumed a 1,100-pound cow in 48 hours. Pete said the grizzly was keeping the other predators away so he could have the cow to himself.

Alec Rosette, cow foreman

One time, Alec, our Native cow foreman, was staying at Yodel camp and sitting near a calf that a bear had killed down along the creek. That spot had the same eerie cathedral effect, with high rock cliffs on both sides and the tall spruce. As he was sitting there just before dark with his old rifle and his back against a tree, a squirrel ran up the tree and scolded him. Alec bolted at the sudden loud sound and ran all the way to the camp, about a mile away. He told himself it had just been a squirrel, but he couldn't convince himself to slow down until he had slammed and bolted the door on the Yodel cabin.

Cougars didn't seem to bother the calves much; they preferred colts and young horses. We had to foal all the colts in the corrals right by the barn or lose them to the cougars. I had always heard that a cougar wouldn't eat anything it hadn't killed, but one particularly bad winter, a family of cougars came into the spot where we put dead animals and ate the horse carcasses.

One summer, while our family was in the back country and Steve Oswald was at the headquarters, he was awakened in the middle of the night by a big disturbance among the dogs down by our house. The commotion was coming from the heeler in a life-and-death struggle with a cougar. When Steve arrived on the scene, the cougar had the heeler's head in its mouth. Steve, being a Mennonite, didn't own a gun, so he hurried to our house, where he knew there was an arsenal. But not being familiar with firearms, he didn't know which bullets went with which gun! Another employee showed up at that point, and together they figured it out. With the loaded shotgun, they ran to the scene of the fight and killed the cougar, but too late to save the badly mangled dog, which died a few days later. It was a sad irony. We had left the dog at home to save her from the back-country wolves, who were famous for killing dogs, only to have her get killed by a cougar at home!

The cougar turned out to be a very old, toothless female driven out of the wilderness by starvation. This is a common occurrence where there are lots of cougars. At the Gang Ranch, one time a cougar came into the headquarters, went into the barn, and perched up in the rafters. When school was over, some children went into the barn to play. Luckily, they saw the cougar and ran for help, and the cougar was quickly dispatched. This turned out to be a very large toothless female. Her hide hung around the Gang for several years.

Sometimes the offender is a young cougar that has never learned to hunt wild game and, at the same time, has lost its fear of man.

We live in Idaho now, and even here we've had cougar attacks in our yard and around the barns. One season, a cat had been hanging around the headquarters of ranches in the area and had killed several goats and turkeys. I gave my wife a pistol to carry on her daily walks for some time. We were all on the alert, and one day it paid off. My son and I were working on an ATV in the yard when we heard a loud rustling in the trees about 20 feet away. We went over to investigate and saw a young cougar with one of our yard cats in his mouth. The yard cat was not a big loss, but of course we weren't going to allow a cougar to have access to our yard.

I sent my son to the house to get a rifle while I kept an eye on the cougar. The cougar remained motionless until Tristan returned with the rifle and I shot the animal. I was shooting through the brush and didn't get a killing shot, but the cougar ran only a short distance into a brush patch. We started into the very thick patch looking for him, but before I had gone ten feet, Tristan said, "Dad, don't put your foot down. You'll be stepping on the cougar's tail!" I stood there on one foot but still couldn't see the cougar. Soon, the cat took off. I tossed the rifle to Tristan, who had a better shot, which he took and killed the cougar.

After we left Empire and moved to Oregon, one more species of wildlife slithered onto our radar. Especially Connie's radar. Our ranch, the Norton, included some mountainous topography, so it was similar to Empire in that aspect. But unlike Empire, it was home to rattlesnakes. Lots of rattlesnakes. In our six years there, we killed 475 rattlers; the count increased considerably when we found a den where they wintered.

My wife harbors a deep and everlasting hatred of rattlesnakes. She is committed to killing every one she sees. A few years ago she was driving our old Suburban up the very winding road to the valley where we live and spotted a rattler on the road. She immediately went into kill mode. I had taught her that if you either tap your brakes or step on the throttle when you run over the snake, it tears them up worse and you are more likely to get a kill. With that in mind, she slowed down until the rear wheels were about to cross the snake and then jammed the throttle to the floor. The Suburban shot forward, but the throttle stuck to the floor. She was gaining speed at this point and wasn't thinking about the key or shifting into neutral. She was just trying to keep the car on the road. Soon the solution hit her and she turned the key off and stopped. You might think she would have forgotten about the snake, but not a chance. She turned around and went clear back to make sure she had a kill. Luckily, the snake was mangled, and she felt all puffed up.

I don't know anyone who sees more rattlers in more odd places than she does. They just seem to gravitate to her. But the attraction is definitely not mutual.

# EPILOGUE

Lincoln City cottage where Tom's earthly journey ended

Tom and I gazed out over the Pacific Ocean. A February storm was blowing. The huge waves seemed as if they might crash over the roof of our little rental cottage. I watched those powerful waves and reflected how much greater God's strength is than man's. I liked to believe I had everything in control, but in reality God's power, not mine, was in control of my life. And that was good, because my faith was about to be tested as it had never been tested before.

We were sipping our coffee, enjoying the beautiful view. We had just finished our morning time of prayer and Bible reading. We had thanked God for this special getaway we were enjoying so much. Tom's heart condition had been slowly getting worse, and he needed a change of pace, a change of scenery, a change of climate. So we had left our Idaho

# EPILOGUE

ranch in the care of our sons, Theron and Tristan, and come to Tom's beloved Oregon Coast for the winter. We were hoping it might help him feel better; the winters seemed to be getting harder on him.

Out of the quiet, Tom asked a question I had never considered.

"What are you going to do when I'm gone?"

My mind froze! I couldn't think. Life without Tom? I couldn't bear to think of it. Our life had been 47 years of one adventure after another.

We started in our twenties on the Colorado ranch where he was the fourth generation. Then we moved the entire operation to Empire Valley, in the wilderness of British Columbia. We spent 12 years in a beautiful, untamed country that offered the challenges and exciting tales you have just read.

Hook family picnic at BC Lake Empire

But Tom was not through with his travels and adventures. We bought a ranch in central Oregon and again moved the whole outfit. We faced new tests, learned new lessons. As our sons became adults and wanted to be part of the ranch, Tom decided a new adventure and ranch was needed. Only a small part of his heart was still working, but he led his family to a new ranch in southern Idaho. As always, he became very involved in the community around us and met the challenges of a new ranch.

Oregon ranch headquarters

All that flashed through my mind as Tom's question hung unanswered.

I sat there looking at him. I didn't know what to say. I'd never heard Tom talk about the end. He was always planning the future. Always coming up with new ideas. Our sons loved to tease him about "Dad's next big idea."

I could not bring myself to answer. Always in the back of my mind I'd vaguely hoped for a miracle cure for his heart. He was only 70. We'd still be together, still madly in love, serving God, and enjoying ranching into our nineties. I was not ready for this. I had no way to know that

## EPILOGUE

Tom would only be with me for a few more days. Somehow God was preparing him for the end of his earthly life, for a new adventure in heaven.

Every day, for many months, Tom had been eagerly blogging on the Cattle Today website. He grew more excited daily, writing about his experiences. More and more readers were added. Many encouraged him to write a book. As he grew weaker, the idea of writing a book seemed to fill his need for a new challenge. He asked his dear friend, Gary Brumbelow, an experienced writer, to help him. Not three weeks earlier, Gary and his wife had come to Lincoln City, and he and Tom had laid the foundation to start working on the book.

But God had other plans.

The morning of February 8, 2011, I arose from bed and found Tom sitting in his chair in the living room. He was facing the beautiful white-capped waves, but he wasn't seeing them. His eyes were closed. He was extremely still and quiet, his only movement the play of his fingers over the waist cord of his pajamas. I tried to talk to him, but he did not respond.

After the 911 call, everything was a blur—ambulance, hospital, staff, doctors, tests. He'd had a massive stroke, they told me, and was totally paralyzed. His weak heart would not survive this trauma, they said. Probably he would not live through the day, I heard them say.

I gazed at my "dragon slayer," lying there paralyzed and dying. It was almost more than I could bear. I was alone. And yet not. I felt God there, close enough to almost touch. So I did the only thing I knew to do. I put one hand in God's hand, and the other in Tom's, and watched as my beloved slowly faded away. And then he was gone.

I left the hospital alone, in a daze. I wasn't sure I could see to drive back to the cottage. But God was with me. Maybe he was driving!

Tom died before anyone else could get there. Somehow I made the difficult calls to family and friends. Our sons had to catch a plane to Portland and then rent a car and drive to the coast. Meanwhile, our good friends Gary and Valerie Brumbelow were already on the road from Portland.

They were the first to arrive. They had been special friends for over 30 years, but I didn't realize how special until they walked in that door.

They stayed with me, and prayed with me, until our sons arrived. When our sons walked in, I felt as if Tom himself were there.

In the following days, several people told me of a premonition that Tom was going. Gary had dreamt he heard Tom calling out to him that very night. Our attorney somehow knew it was coming a few days before Tom passed away. And when our five-year-old grandson, Timothy, was told that his "papa" had died, he said he already knew. God had told him. Yes, in his mercy, God was trying to prepare us for this difficult loss.

As for Tom's question, "What will you do when I'm gone?": it nearly paralyzed me to hear him ask it, but I guess I knew the answer all along. I would stay close to our sons and their families. We would continue with our ranch in Idaho. That's as close to Tom as I could be.

He didn't get to finish his last dream of writing a book. But I'm glad we can share his blogs with you. I hope you will be encouraged by them to seek and fulfill the dreams God has given you for your life. You won't be disappointed. His plan for you is perfect.

Connie Hook,<br>
Nampa, Idaho<br>
March 28, 2017

# IMAGES

Connie, Theron, and Connie's dad, Kenneth Longaker, fording Relay Creek

Driving cattle at Oregon ranch

# MOUNTAIN RANCH AT THE END OF THE ROAD

Horse in Relay line cabin

# IMAGES

Empire Valley ranch scene

Empire Valley ranch scene

# MOUNTAIN RANCH AT THE END OF THE ROAD

**Looking north along the Fraser**

**Rugged topography along the Fraser**

# IMAGES

Fraser River sage country

Alec driving team and wagon at Empire

# MOUNTAIN RANCH AT THE END OF THE ROAD

Alec driving team and wagon

Branding day at Empire

# IMAGES

Branding day at Empire

Tom in corral at Oregon ranch

# MOUNTAIN RANCH AT THE END OF THE ROAD

Tom roping at Oregon ranch

Tom and Tristan with Oregon buck

IMAGES

Tom with Oregon buck

Hooks and Brumbelows, 1980

# MOUNTAIN RANCH AT THE END OF THE ROAD

Jim and Connie Penturf

Tom and sons

IMAGES

Tom and sons

Theron and Tristan Hook

Hook family 2002, Idaho

# IMAGES

Hook family 2014, Idaho

Tom Hook

## APPENDIX A

# RANCHING IN CANADA VS. THE U.S.

I have been asked to give my impressions of the differences between ranching in Canada and in the U.S.

As for ranching in Canada, I really can't give a knowledgeable description of anything outside the central western ranch area of British Columbia. The area where we lived and operated was called the Cariboo,[11] and we were in the most western area of that region. The area immediately to the north is the Chilcotin, a large, rolling, mainly pine-covered plateau with a lot of long, somewhat boggy meadows. The surface mud there is locally referred to as "Loon be nice." Another famous saying in the Chilcotin is, "Have you seen my horses?" That's probably due to the shortage of fencing in a very large area. That very large plateau has lots of ranches, and the people who inhabit them are a truly strong and unique bunch.

The summers there are short and the winters long, snowy, and cold. The hay is almost all native grass, a lot of it pretty coarse.

Along the Fraser River and some of the Chilcotin are much lower bench lands with a very different climate that allows alfalfa and some corn for silage. The steep sides of these rivers

Neighbor's hay meadows near Empire

---

[11]"An intermontane region of British Columbia along a plateau stretching from the Fraser Canyon to the Cariboo Mountains. The name is a reference to the caribou that were once abundant in the region." Wikipedia

provide late fall, winter, and early spring grazing. Where these two rivers converge, south of Williams Lake, is a large reserve for California bighorn sheep. This is probably the most famous herd anywhere and has been the source for many herds across Canada and the U.S. The rams coming out of there are beyond incredible. Farther to the south, after leaving Big Bar and Lillooet, the Fraser enters a very steep canyon inhabited only by mountain goats and bighorn sheep.

Fraser north of Empire

As to comparisons to similar areas in the U.S., I would say this area in Owyhee County, Idaho, is colder, with moderately more snow and a lot more ice. The Be Nice Canyon area along the Snake River between Idaho and Oregon would be similar but warmer, with the snow cover not lasting as long. The Imnaha River in that area would also be quite similar. There is an area along the Columbia River between Washington and Oregon that would also qualify. This last area would lie south of Goldendale, Washington. The hills along the Thompson River around

Kamloops, B.C., would be similar, as would a small part of the Columbia River in southeast B.C.

These areas are all really quite similar and are my favorite areas for ranching, due to the differences in elevation and the advantage of having a large variety of seasons and grasses and the opportunity to graze rotationally, with some pasture going toward fresh grass nearly all the time.

We chose this ranch in Idaho because it promised 365 days of grazing for a third of the cattle, mountain living, and end-of-the-road tranquility. Since we have been here we have been able to rent winter grazing for the rest of the cows, so a lifetime dream has been fulfilled.

The most famous grass for this lower country in Idaho was the native blue bunch grass, or Idaho fescue. It was uniquely suited for winter grazing, as its feed value increased when it matured and dried. When it was growing, the feed value was pretty low.

We do still put up about 1,500 tons of hay. So we are breaking the Pharo rules of low inputs. However, almost all our hay is sold to what we affectionately call "critter people." That's another difference between here and operating in Canada. Critter people have a small acreage, with lots of different kinds of animals. The range of animals is astounding to us, from rabbits to horses and everything in between. One day a woman called and wanted to buy a big bale of alfalfa for her rabbits. When I asked, "How many rabbits do you have?" she said "One!" I wondered out loud if she realized how long it would take one rabbit to eat 1,000 pounds of hay.

Another couple came for hay for her goats. Her husband had come along very reluctantly. When I asked him what line of work he was in, he said he was a corporate jet pilot. I asked him how he had gotten into the goat business, since that seemed so different from corporate piloting. At this point, the couple began to yell at one another. I could hear them yelling clear out on to the highway as they left.

At the present time we raise Roundup Ready alfalfa, which for us is a fantastic crop. We can just spray the fields with Roundup and all the unwanted weeds and grasses are gone. We are especially interested in eliminating Medusa Head, a particularly nasty grass that is silicon based and unpalatable to livestock. You can clearly see any spots you miss, because the weeds really stick up. This variety of alfalfa has been banned for several years, but the legality of that ban will be decided by the Supreme Court in June. Hopefully the ban will be lifted and we will once again plant, as our stands are getting fairly old. Even though they are old they are still in pretty good shape because of the lack of competition from the weeds. Until we used it we never knew how much the weeds were affecting the stands.

Idaho ranch headquarters

Our Idaho ranch is the center of an area studied by the Agricultural Research Service (ARS), a department of the USDA. This group measures every drop of rain and snow that falls, either through their weirs or directly at their sites. All the National Weather Service projections come from this data.

A few years ago they agreed to do a controlled burn of about 300 acres of our pasture. Before they burned, they wanted to measure the cattle grazing patterns. To accomplish that, they provided us with GPS collars to put on our cows. At that time collars cost $7,000 each; now they are about $700. They loaned us 15 collars, we put them on the cows and turned them out in the pasture scheduled for burning. The collars were set to ping every 15 minutes. At that rate they would last about a month. This was all tracked and recorded on a computer. At the end of the experiment, they generated a map on which the pings showed up as dots on the screen. Each cow was represented by a different color dot. We could track their movements 24/7.

It made for a real neat map that told some interesting stories about those old bossies. One old cow walked a long way to a gate every several days, apparently to see if the gate was open. When a dot didn't move over a period of time, it meant a cow had lost her collar or had died.

After working with the USDA people for several years, I can affirm they have no knowledge of private economics. A couple of weeks ago we found some cattle still out on the mountain in the snow. After we drove them home, we were visiting with some of the USDA people and they said, "Oh yeah, we have been seeing those cows up there for a couple months." I don't think it ever occurred to them to tell us. And they wonder why we are very reluctant to give them new access, etc. Being a good neighbor is a concept totally foreign to bureaucrats!

It has always seemed to me, wherever we have lived, that the early snows are dry and just blow around all winter. The biggest benefit from them is the drifts that are formed on the peaks.

Here in Idaho it is much the same, except our peaks are much lower (under 6,000 feet). An early snow here often is followed by a warm rain that runs most of the snow out, as happened last week. We had a big runoff for several days, but the drifts stayed and, given the rain and subsequent freeze, they are now totally ice. The most beneficial snows here come after January 15. These contain more moisture and don't melt out. Up here on the mountain ranch we generally start irrigating in early March, as our creeks usually run out in June. We get one cutting of grass hay.

We are going to try something new this year. We are going to pasture the meadows during the month of April, hoping the grass grows back enough to produce in June. Since we have to feed during April, we hope any loss in production from the grazing will be offset by the smaller amount of hay we will need to feed. We tried one meadow last year and were very pleased.

We live in a sagebrush high-desert area, where they say the annual precipitation is about 10 inches. However our summer and fall pastures only five miles away get 38 inches.

## APPENDIX B

# CATTLE BREEDING & BLOODLINES

My family has operated a commercial, open-range cattle business for 145 years. In 1908, my great-grandfather purchased a number of registered Horned Hereford females as well as bulls. They finally turned those animals' progeny into the commercial herd in the early '30s. When I came on the management scene in the mid-'50s the dwarfism thing was in full swing. We had used Thornton Ranch Triumphs out of a Denver champion or class winner, Baca Dukes, from the St. Luis Maria Baca Grant ranch, and Alpine Dominos from Trails End Ranch. They were all carriers, or "dirty," although we actually had very few dwarf calves. While looking for some "clean" bulls we ran across a CK bull that we loved. That led us to the CK Ranch, where we purchased bulls for several years to clean up the mess and have a source large enough to pick a number of bulls from. CK Ranch was advertising 222 bulls in their sale.

At this time we decided to re-establish a purebred herd to produce our own bulls. The theory was: Where else could we pick the top calves every year for our bull needs? The fad was still for small cattle, so we bought some heifers from Miller and Martensen from Hayden, Colorado, and a couple of bulls. They proved to be too small and were prone to the brisket problem. One bull from them never sired a calf that could reach one year of age. They were a failure and mistake.

From that point, we went to Franklin Nash (see Appendix C for more about this remarkable friend) for some females and bulls that worked great, except for the disposition. We owned quite a few herd bulls in partnership with Franklin. At this time we also used Superior E468, who was straight Anxiety 4th or "in the temple." He was a great bull with length, muscle, and thickness, and did us a world of good except for the udders, which sloped too much from front to rear.

Next came several bulls from Carl Martin of Menard, Texas. Carl was as much of a maverick as Ferry Carpenter, or more. He was one of the most decorated veterans from World War II. He had basically Anxiety 4th cattle but they were not straight enough to be in the temple.

Carl Martin had a great ranch just out of Menard. Carl took me on almost like a son for about 10 years in the late '60s and early '70s. I visited his ranch every year, and he came to mine a couple of times. The first three years I spent just trying to convince him to sell me a bull. I guess he thought I was a spy from the AHA crowd he hated. He finally let me have Prince Blanchard 170, a Mischief Return, Lamplighter. 170 was pretty feminine but really bred outstanding females; we still have lots of descendants from him. Later we got Blanchard Lad 211 and Blanchard Lad 212. These two were much more masculine but still are the foundation sires of our present-day females.

During the earlier years of this time the dwarfism thing took an interesting turn. The AHA decided to clean up the mess by identifying all the carriers by a pedigree check. The other alternative was a progeny test accomplished by breeding a bull to at least 15 of his own daughters and then, if there were no dwarfs, the bull could be called clean. Both methods were successful, but the AHA never sanctioned the progeny test, which left a cloud over the cattle that were cleared that way. The argument raged for years over the merits of both methods, much like the Polled Hereford argument of today, with just as much passion and unrelenting animosity. Our cattle were pedigree clean, but many of our friends went the other way. I got caught once when I purchased some cows that were progeny clean, but I had to put them in the commercials.

We acquired some bulls from Montana that were Axtell bred and had more size than what we had had. One of the bulls was a full brother of his 80th bull that he relied on so much in his later years.

Next came a son of Chris Jacobsen's big cow and later a full brother to him from the Hunter herd dispersion. These were pretty large bulls, with the one from Chris being much larger. These cattle produced a lot of females for us.

# CATTLE BREEDING & BLOODLINES

At this time we moved from Colorado to British Columbia, taking our purebreds with us. We had a terrible time with the blue-tongue testing required by Canada Customs (which was actually no more than a trade barrier by the Canadians).

This move forced a change in our breeding strategy because of the colder weather. The Martin cattle just wouldn't do under those conditions but, needless to say, the Becker cattle and the Jacobsen cattle did great. Every generation from the straight Martin animal did better than the last. They were also a very different phenotype than the Canadian cattle around us. For commercial cattle, we bought an entire herd of local cows we called the TJ cows. They were great range cows and moved right in and went to work. The only problem we had with them was getting their daughters to rebreed after their first calf, but this was the fault of the ranch and the environment.

At this time I had to learn to market under the B.C. conditions, which were complicated by the distance to the feedlots in Alberta and Ontario. We needed to sell cattle in load lots to avoid piecing loads together for the long haul east. Years earlier, while working in the Denver carloads for M&M, I got experience marketing uniform cattle, so I decided to use that approach. Every September, Kamloops had a 20,000-head auction called the Panorama. We consigned several hundred steers to that sale. We sorted them in very uniform load lots and instructed the auction barn to run them right off the trucks into the sale ring. To our surprise, they topped the sale, confirming even further that uniformity was money in my pocket. This drove our purebred program from then on. We needed about fifty bulls for turnout; at one time we had fifty 3/4 to 15/16 brothers to be used on the commercial cows. Without our own purebred cows, we could never had gotten that done.

One of the buyers of our Panorama loads was a fine old cattle buyer, Lew Williams, who took us under his arm. From the time we met him, Lew bought everything we sold and did all of our order buying as well. One fall, when we had several hundred calves in a feedlot in Kamloops, Lew asked me if we would let him use small numbers of our calves to fill out some big loads headed east. He guaranteed a premium and also promised to buy what we had left at the end of the shipping season. We agreed and did very well with this arrangement. One time we had a few one-eyed and crippled heifers left. Lew said he wanted to send them to a little Saturday pig market sale that did very well on ditch-bank calves. We agreed, and the local pig farmer hauled them about 60 miles to the sale. When Lew got the check, he called me and we had a great laugh: those heifers had averaged nearly $1.34 a pound, a truly remarkable price at that time. We figured sympathy from the ditch-bank people had influenced the price!

## APPENDIX C

# FRANKLIN NASH

I promised an entire appendix devoted to Franklin Nash. I really knew an awful lot about Franklin, as we were partners and friends for over 20 years.

Together we started a bull test that we called Hereford Bulls, Inc. We operated that endeavor for several years in the early '70s with the help of a young Oklahoma State University grad, Jim Penturf, who was without a doubt the smartest cattleman I ever knew. Franklin said the young man had a mind like a steel trap. Franklin and I traveled together all the time and bought bulls together at dispersions, as he was always looking for a good out cross and I enjoyed the trip and conversations. He had a hard time sleeping, so rather than wake me up he would take the TV into the bathroom, set it on the tub and sit down on the toilet to watch. We always laughed that at that time of night he was probably watching the color test pattern.

Franklin had some neighbors—the Dilleys, who were also friends and customers—that did most of his horse cattle work for him. They were as good at that as I have ever seen. One time they were helping him put his herd bulls out with the cows when one old bull refused to go and really got on the fight. They tried for several hours to get the bull out but finally had to give up. Franklin told them not to worry, he would take care of it the next day. The next day he took his old Dodge Power Wagon and hit the bull in the ribs, which toppled him over. Franklin then drove the Power Wagon right up on top of the downed bull, climbed out of the truck, hooked a chain around the bull's horns, and dragged him to the proper pasture, where he proceeded to die. I am not sure what bull it was, as the incident happened before my involvement with Franklin and was relayed to me by the Dilleys.

I owned several Nash bulls either outright or in partnership with Franklin. They were 110, 125, 155, and Golden Advance. One time, as I was moving 110 from one corral to the next, he whirled around and pinned me to the fence. Luckily for me, his horns were high enough that they hit the poles in the fence, leaving room for me. His horns actually protected me from being crushed by his head. This caught me completely by surprise, as he had never shown those tendencies before and even at the time was totally quiet.

Another time, when I unloaded him from a trailer into the cow pasture, he whirled around again. That time I was ready for him and managed to get up on the trailer. Needless to say, we both quit using the bull after that. Believe me, they could be tough. I have heard from others who knew the cattle very well that the Arrow bloodline fixed that particular problem.

We also bought several bulls from breeders that had used his old 068 bull and a few others.

Another time we were in Dalhart, Texas, overnight on our way to Amarillo, where he bought an Onward Herd bull. Franklin was always up and out earlier than me, and he would invariably go out, start our car, race the engine, and sit there reading an early newspaper.

This particular morning we had another friend of mine along, and we dreamed up the bright idea of calling the motel manager and complaining about an obnoxious driver out front of our unit, disturbing our rest. We peeked out the window and watched the lady motel manager come marching out and really ream Franklin out. We were dying with laughter and had a tough time keeping quiet at breakfast when he told us about his misfortune. We never did tell him just what had transpired.

When we were running Hereford Bulls a young man I'll call Al lived in a house at the feedlot. He had kept a mangy old German shepherd for some time, and then he got a blue heeler from us (which would prove to be a much more useful dog). The old dog kept teaching the young dog bad habits, so one day Al shot the shepherd. He didn't have time right then to haul the dead dog off, so he left him lying there. The younger dog missed his friend and slept up against him all day, so all the fleas moved off the dead dog onto the heeler. At this time Franklin arrived on the scene to do the monthly books. Franklin hated dogs and never had one, but for some unknown reason he let the heeler go into the house with him. Franklin proceeded to sit at the dining room table, and the heeler, feeling lonely, kept loving up to Franklin, who, absorbed in his books and not thinking about what was happening, kept scratching the dog. Needless to say, a good portion of the fleas transferred to Franklin. Later, on his way home in his big black Cadillac with white upholstery, Franklin began to itch. Once he figured out why he was itching so bad, it didn't take him long to figure out where the fleas came from.

Another time, Franklin had his old pet 086 bull out somewhere for display for a Hereford tour in a small corral. Franklin was very anxious to show him off and demonstrate that he was not mean. 086 had a look on his face that said "stay away," which everyone did. But Franklin wanted everyone to know how gentle 086 was. I was very anxious to see how he did it, and it was something to watch. First, Franklin took a long time just to get up to the backside of the bull. Having achieved that, he give the critter a very slight tap. The bull never moved, and Franklin retreated posthaste. To what degree he convinced anyone was another matter.

Franklin Nash had many sides to his personality, and broad interests. For one thing, he was a big fan of classical music. He was very involved with the local fine arts committee and always had season tickets to their programs in his home town. He rarely missed a concert. One fall, he insisted that my wife and I accompany him and his wife to the winter concerts. I guess he thought that I could use some culture to smooth out my redneck tendencies. I was a country music fan and followed Merle Haggard, Charlie Pride, and Tammy Wynette. We went, but after several concerts he decided we weren't as enthralled as he had hoped, so he kindly dropped the idea. I noticed the concerts were not very well attended, so maybe he was working on a membership quota.

Another side to Franklin was his fondness for agate. He loved making belt buckles and bolo ties out of some of the most beautiful agate in the world. He even took a course at a local community college to learn the art of silversmithing. He was really very good, and I still have several belt buckles and bolos that he made. I treasure them highly. He also had the most extensive collection of agate and arrowheads I have ever seen, though my experience is somewhat limited in that area.

Another facet was his love of still-life paintings. He became acquainted with a local artist who was very talented. Franklin really got me interested in this man's paintings. Our house is filled with his art, and we get lots of compliments on their beauty.

Speaking of art, Franklin got acquainted with an artist who was incarcerated at the state prison in our home town. Franklin wanted him to paint some pictures of his cattle from photographs. We were so impressed that I even commissioned him to do a picture of Carl Martin's old herd bull as a gift for Carl. The guy was totally amazing. In fact, he had been convicted of forgery! He could write, with either hand, sentences that you had to hold up to a mirror to read. He could also write a sentence backwards with his right hand and the same sentence forward with his left hand at the same time.

I have always been grateful for the diversity Franklin brought to my life.

Franklin was absolutely one of the most honest men I ever knew. He belongs with some others in the cattle business such as Carl Martin, Jack Koster (from Canada), Jim Penturf, and our son. Our son is almost too much so. When we try to sell a ranch or anything, we all laugh that we have to keep the lookers away from him, or he will tell them all the faults and bad points first. He would be a disaster around a purebred operation. On the other hand, when he goes with me to look at any purchase, he quietly stands off to one side and then, at some time, sidles over to me and points out the faults of whatever we are appraising.

Each story about Franklin triggers another fond memory. He used to buy a lot of hay from us to feed his young bulls. He always wanted us to deliver the hay and stack it in the lofts of his several scattered barns. This was a lot of work, as we had to use a small truck to get into place next to these barns. The hay had to be thrown into the loft and then packed to the back of the loft. This was no small chore and we certainly wouldn't have done it for anyone else.

Franklin also had several outhouses, all on concrete floors, fairly large and frequently used. Since Franklin was always making his feed rounds, it was important that his privies be kept in very good condition. One time the truck driver, who also had a great sense of humor, agreed to a scheme to fill an outhouse with bales. Franklin had always said to "fill everything to the brim" and so we thought we should oblige. This particular outhouse at an outlying ranch was a nice large one, and we packed it to the roof.

For a long time we didn't hear a word from Franklin and grew somewhat apprehensive. Several weeks later, after staying away from Franklin, for obvious reasons, I received a letter in the mail. It was from Franklin. In the letter was a picture of some long johns hanging on a clothesline, badly soiled on the rear flap. He had included a note that said "drastic circumstances cause drastic problems." No other word about the incident was ever mentioned between us. I could just picture Franklin chuckling over his response.

## APPENDIX D

# SURVIVING AT EMPIRE

Tom by fence above hydro plant

In Chapter 3, I described the hydroelectric system we installed at Empire. We also had a backup diesel generator for outages or when the temperature dipped under -10. Below that temperature, our creek would freeze up so hard there was not enough water to generate power for the refrigerators, etc., in the houses. Even at -40, enough water would pass through the turbine to power engine heaters on a couple of trucks or tractors. But the low voltage would have burned up an electric motor in a few minutes.

I had been told to look for a Lister air-cooled diesel generator that turned at 1,200 rpm. At this slow speed that old engine would last several years before overhaul (which could be accomplished right where the engine sat). It was also very efficient on fuel and totally reliable, so that is what we found and installed. After 12 years of using this generator as a backup at least two months of the year, we fell in love with these Listers. Their ability to start in very cold weather was truly a blessing. If the temp dropped to -10 or less we needed a backup generator very quickly, or everything would freeze. When we installed backup generators at our current ranches, we decided again to use Listers, partly out of nostalgia and partly out of the knowledge of these engines. I found them on eBay and had them trucked here on U-ship. If the consumption table holds true, we should use less than a half a gallon per hour. So if we run them just two hours per day, a 300-gallon fuel tank should last around 300 days. These are smaller 5kW models that will run our homesteads just fine. These engines can take an overload for quite some time. The good thing about them is that they cost much less than the new Hondas or Yamahas of the same size. These engines aren't hard to start with the hand crank because they have a compression release that makes them easy to turn over by hand. The original models were the CS models; the CS stood for cold start.

The Honda or Yamaha generators are more costly but also work great. As I mentioned, we found we could get by with just a couple of hours of electricity per day, say from 7 to 8 in the morning and 6 to 7 in the evening. This greatly reduces fuel consumption and extends the usefulness of your system if you can't replenish the fuel supply. We learned this at Empire right after we moved in. The old Cat generator that came with the ranch was on its last legs, as it consumed a gallon of oil and a lots of fuel every day. To extend the life of the Cat while we were putting in our hydro, we reverted to the two-hours-per-day system. If you are careful about opening the fridge and freezer, they will cool just fine when run two hours a day.

We have lived for 33 years, more or less, in this survival mode, not necessarily to prepare for disaster but out of necessity. Nearly all of the ranches we have owned were at the end of the road and very remote. When we bought Empire it had only diesel-powered electricity.

Back then, the cost of generating power from diesel was about $25,000 per year; today that price would be closer to $70,000. Not many ranches can handle that kind of expense just to power the houses.

Since people have asked about the design and installation of these things, I will share some observations and ideas about self-sufficiency, preparedness, and survival. You can't be prepared for everything, so you need to prioritize your needs in case of an emergency.

Providing for water is the most critical. Within hours of losing electrical power you will need water. You have three possibilities: 1) Gravity pressure, 2) Windmill from a cistern, or 3) Sun or wind generation to power a pump. We have always been lucky enough to have (potential if not actual) gravity-pressured water to the house. You can develop a surface-fed spring fairly easily, and if is slightly higher than your house, you are in business, except for the need to purify the surface water. We are using such a system now, and are trying a 12-volt pump to boost pressure. The pump is an off-the-shelf ATV sprayer pump with about a 5 gpm capacity. So far, it has lasted nearly a year, but the next test is to try this pump in a well to see if it can draw water from a well 15 to 20 feet deep. If it has enough suction, we can set up a solar-powered battery charger and have a totally self-sufficient water supply. To save the battery, we would need to install a switch to turn the pump off when we're not using water.

First, you need to filter out particles. We use a five-micron filter available at stores like Lowe's. Next in the series, you need a carbon filter for odors, and some chemicals, also available at Lowe's. Finally, but very important, is a filter for bacteria. We use an ultraviolet light filter that will kill any bacteria we might encounter. These are available on the Internet; we use the Steri-Light filter. It consists of an ultraviolet lamp inside a stainless-steel tube. This three-step system should purify water anywhere, unless it's contaminated with commercial chemicals. The cost should be about $300 for all three filters. Ours uses power from the public utility, but when that goes out, even though the gravity pressurization would supply water to the house, our water would not be safe to drink. To get around this all-too-frequent occurrence, we put in a deep-cycle marine battery that, through a common car battery inverter, powers the ultraviolet lamp. We hooked a common small battery charger between the power grid power source and the battery to keep the battery fully charged. When the power goes out, the light is still powered by the battery and our water is still being treated. The battery will power the light for about 24 hours. Next, we should add a solar-powered battery charger to the system for full self-sufficiency.

The second priority is refrigeration. Those of us on farms or ranches think that we have a food source, and we do, but meat needs refrigeration most of the year. A calf or steer will spoil before you can eat all of it. Sheep, pigs, and chickens are smaller, so they can be consumed maybe before spoiling. Another method for cooling is to place an old refrigerator under a source of cool water so the water flows down over the outside of the fridge.

I won't go into heating, because you may have quite some time to prepare after the power fails and there is a wealth of information out there on that already. The reason I am discussing the items above is the emergency situation you may find yourself in after the power fails. You will need water very quickly, so that is the one thing you need to prepare for beforehand. Refrigeration allows some time for preparation, but not water.

My boys tease me that I am not preparing for an outage but Armageddon instead.

# INDEX

## A

Alberta 36, 51, 52, 55, 57, 91, 106, 151
alfalfa 24, 60, 144, 146

## B

bales 59, 156
bear 6, 61, 62, 70, 76, 92, 95, 110, 111, 112, 113, 114, 115, 116, 117, 118, 119, 120, 121, 122, 127
Bighorn 58, 111, 112, 145
Bloodlines 149
brand 13, 68, 83, 86, 136, 137
Breeding 32, 149
British Columbia 6, 14, 20, 33, 74, 127, 144, 151
bull 9, 51, 53, 55, 56, 65, 66, 68, 149, 150, 151, 153, 154, 155, 156

## C

calf 10, 72, 89, 112, 122, 149, 151, 161
calves 51, 57, 60, 62, 78, 86, 112, 118, 123, 149, 151, 152
calving 9, 11, 84, 85, 95, 112, 118
Canada 14, 20, 32, 33, 42, 45, 61, 62, 89, 90, 92, 144, 145, 146, 147, 148, 151, 156
Colorado 6, 12, 13, 14, 15, 18, 19, 27, 43, 45, 49, 51, 59, 64, 91, 92, 110, 127, 149, 157
colts 123
cowboys 10, 29, 31, 32, 36, 38, 50, 51, 65, 66, 67, 74, 75, 77, 81, 83, 84, 86, 89, 97, 98, 110, 111, 115,
cows 6, 14, 15, 16, 27, 30, 32, 33, 35, 41, 51, 53, 54, 55, 58, 60, 61, 62, 70, 86, 97, 146, 147, 148, 150, 151, 153
coyote 58, 62, 109, 114

## D

deer 57, 62, 109

## E

eagle 6, 61, 109, 111, 112, 113

## F

feed 13, 14, 49, 54, 55, 56, 59, 60, 64, 69, 70, 74, 78, 109, 112, 146, 148, 151, 154, 156
fence 24, 29, 34, 58, 68, 71, 77, 92, 95, 101, 154, 158
Fraser 14, 23, 26, 28, 33, 40, 49, 54, 55, 56, 63, 64, 65, 71, 74, 80, 90, 91, 103, 108, 112, 134, 135, 144, 145,

## G

goat 42, 124, 145, 146
grass 14, 35, 51, 57, 58, 60, 85, 111, 144, 146, 148

# INDEX

graze 13, 49, 60, 111, 146
grizzly / grizzlies 6, 7, 76, 111, 114, 116, 117, 119, 121, 122
grouse 110

## H

hay 12, 13, 14, 27, 30, 39, 45, 48, 49, 50, 54, 55, 56, 57, 58, 59, 60, 69, 71, 77, 101, 144, 146, 148, 156
heifer 9, 10, 11, 16, 27, 51, 52, 71, 72, 112, 118, 149, 152
herd 13, 27, 33, 50, 51, 53, 55, 69, 109, 145, 149, 150, 151, 153, 154, 156
Hereford 51, 56, 149, 150, 153, 154, 155
horse / horseback 12, 13, 16, 28, 29, 31, 32, 36, 39, 40, 42, 50, 56, 57, 58, 59, 62, 65, 66, 67, 69, 75, 76, 77, 78, 80, 83, 84, 86, 87, 88, 89, 98, 106, 112, 113, 114, 116, 117, 120, 121, 123, 132, 144, 146, 153
hunt 33, 37, 40, 42, 69, 71, 80, 81, 98, 110, 111, 113, 117, 118, 119, 120, 121, 123

## L

lamb 11, 112

## M

meadow 13, 45, 48, 49, 60, 77, 94, 114, 116, 117, 144, 148
mice /mouse 119, 120
miner 35, 36, 58
moose 69, 84, 111
mountain 6, 11, 12, 13, 16, 18, 24, 29, 30, 33, 39, 41, 43, 44, 45, 48, 49, 57, 60, 61, 69, 74, 80, 81, 83, 87, 92, 93, 94, 97, 98, 110, 120, 124, 144, 145, 146, 148

## N

Native 6, 20, 29, 31, 36, 39, 40, 66, 67, 69, 70, 73, 74, 76, 79, 83, 84, 85, 86, 91, 92, 93, 94, 95, 96, 98, 99, 101, 102, 104, 106, 108, 111, 113, 115, 116, 119, 121, 122

## O

Oregon 7, 8, 38, 80, 81, 96, 124, 127, 128, 131, 137, 138, 139, 145

## P

pasture 14, 29, 35, 39, 40, 49, 51, 57, 58, 60, 62, 68, 71, 77, 117, 120, 146, 147, 148, 153, 154
purebred 15, 27, 28, 45, 51, 55, 66, 68, 96, 149, 151, 156

## R

rabbit 146
rams 111, 145
range 6, 13, 29, 30, 31, 35, 41, 50, 57, 70, 71, 73, 76, 118, 146, 149, 151
rattlesnakes 16, 124
roping 83, 84, 88, 116, 138

## S

salmon 108, 109
sheep 33, 58, 111, 112, 121,

# INDEX

145, 161
  steer 14, 51, 56, 57, 58, 111, 151, 161
  summer 13, 27, 30, 31, 35, 36, 45, 47, 51, 56, 60, 61, 65, 72, 75, 76, 77, 83, 97, 99, 102, 107, 110, 116, 123, 144, 148

## T

trout 110

## W

Washington 28, 46, 48, 51, 145

wilderness 6, 7, 89, 123, 127
winter 13, 14, 18, 27, 31, 33, 36, 37, 39, 40, 45, 47, 49, 50, 51, 56, 57, 58, 60, 61, 69, 70, 71, 83, 86, 92, 96, 99, 100, 103, 109, 120, 121, 123, 124, 127, 144, 145, 146, 148, 155
wolf / wolves 6, 7, 58, 71, 111, 123

## Y

yearling 51, 56, 57, 62, 63, 67, 117

# BOOK REVIEWS

"I thoroughly enjoyed reading Mountain Ranch at the End of the Road. It is a must read, especially for those of similar vintage who can relate the stories to the adventures and misadventures in our own lives. Each story brings back memories long since forgotten. Old and young alike will find the book an inspiration to look for and pursue opportunity even when it is necessary to discover new ways to achieve success. It has been an honor for me to review this book and learn much more about the life lived by my friend Tom Hook."

**Dr. Chad C Gibson, PhD, Range Sciences**

"The Hook's commitment to God and family, their adventurous spirit, and love of a good challenge shine brightly in this book. We always enjoyed Tom's stories of their time in Canada and reading them felt like listening to Tom again."

**Tim & Rosa Maria Lowry, ranchers**

"The only let down with Tom Hook's writing was its being cut short by his death. The manuscript was so interesting that I couldn't put it down."

**Michael F Hanley IV, rancher, historian, and winner of the 1973 Cowboy Hall of Fame Western Heritage Wrangler Award**

"Mountain Ranch at the End of the Road is a personal story about a fourth-generation ranching family who leave a "sure fire" ranch in Colorado, to a "not-so-sure" ranch in the mountains of British Columbia, Canada. Praying earnestly for God's leading, Tom, and Connie Hook and their boys, loaded up all their belongings, including machinery, horses & mounted up for the Empire Ranch. Mountain Ranch is well worth reading for the entire family."

**Pastor Jack E Miller, author of Tough and Tender, a cowboy poetry book.**

# other titles by Hancock House Publishers

**The Incredible Gang Ranch**
Dale Alsager
9780888392114
5½ x 8½, sc, 448 pp
**$29.95**

The true story of Empire's neighboring farm and Canada's largest ranch- *The Incredible Gang Ranch.*

**Rhymes on the Range & Rhymes and Damn Lies**
Mike Puhallo et al
9780888396242
9780888393685
5½ x 8½, sc, 64pp
**$9.95**

**Gold Creeks & Ghost Towns**
Bill Barlee
9780888399885
8½ x 11, sc, 192 pp
**$24.95**

**Frontier Forts & Posts**
Kenneth Perry
9780888395986
8½ x 11 sc, 96 pp
**$16.95**

**Ralph Edwards of Lonesome Lake**
Ed Gould & Ralph Edwards
9780888391001
5½ x 8½, sc, 296 pp
**$19.95**

**Descent Into Madness**
Vernon Frolick
9780888390264
5½ x 8½, sc, 361 pp
**$24.95**

**Amber River: a guide to unique pubs on Vancouver Island**
Glen Cowley
9780888390752
5½ x 8½, sc, 226 pp
**$29.95**

**Outposts & Bushplanes**
Bruce Lamb
9780888395566
5½ x 8½, sc, 208 pp
**$17.95**

**Hancock House Publishers**
19313 0 Ave, Surrey, BC V3Z 9R9
www.hancockhouse.com
sales@hancockhouse.com
1-800-938-1114

www.ingramcontent.com/pod-product-compliance
Lightning Source LLC
Chambersburg PA
CBHW070944230426
43666CB00011B/2557